"Our churches desperately need to move beyond the spiritual infancy of merely wading in the shallows and begin to plunge with determined dedication into spiritual ocean depths. Spiritual formation has emerged as a great need of the hour, but biblically grounded, Christ-focused spiritual formation is paramount. Graham Joseph Hill has expertly crafted such a resource to assist in meeting this great need. May it be warmly embraced and bear much fruit."

—PAUL QUICKE,
lead pastor, Morley Baptist Church

"I always walked into Graham Joseph Hill's seminary classes with a heart full of expectation. Now, opening his books evokes that same excitement. This new devotion is a deep river of spiritual insight. Dive in and be refreshed."

—TIM KAY,
senior pastor, Thornleigh Community Baptist Church

"It is with great joy that I offer my wholehearted endorsement for this daily devotional. Graham Joseph Hill's deeply insightful reflections take the profound truths of Scripture and present them in a wonderfully helpful, accessible form. This inspiring devotional work is a blessing, and I look forward to the subsequent volumes."

—NICK SCOTT,
senior pastor, Mount Pleasant Baptist Church

"This devotional is for you if you want a concise, thoughtful engagement with the Bible. Graham Joseph Hill's deep theological reflections challenge the reader to consider how this book of the Bible impacts us today. I have found this to be an excellent yet challenging companion in my daily reflection time."

—SALLY PIM,
intercultural team member, Baptist Mission Australia

"Graham Joseph Hill's book of devotionals is a refreshing well of rediscovery into the Bible. No topic is overlooked here; from the depth of sin to the absurdity of God's grace freely given, serious treatment has been given to the overarching themes of the Christian faith. Surprising little details we may have overlooked have been captured brilliantly. This is a stellar contribution to what will no doubt be a series of devotionals that will impact a generation of believers with the awe, hope, and promise of God and his Word."

—ED DIVINE,
church relationship manager, Baptist World Aid

"In a world of potential distractions, Graham Joseph Hill skilfully and sensitively encourages us to draw near to God so that we, too, might hear the heartbeat of the living God speaking through Scripture in the context of God's redemptive story. Graham's devotions are profoundly beautiful to read, deeply encouraging, and sufficiently challenging in application and as a teaching resource for a broad spectrum of people, whether they be an enquirer or a seasoned disciple."

—ANN CLEWS,
follower of Jesus Christ

Mark

Daily Devotions with Jesus

Mark

Receiving Redemption and Fulfilling Divine Promise: A Fifty-Day Devotional

GRAHAM JOSEPH HILL

WIPF & STOCK · Eugene, Oregon

MARK
Receiving Redemption and Fulfilling Divine Promise:
A Fifty-Day Devotional

Wipf & Stock Publications
An Imprint of Wipf and Stock Publishers
199 W. 8th Ave., Suite 3
Eugene, OR 97401

www.wipfandstock.com

PAPERBACK ISBN: 979-8-3852-1417-4
HARDCOVER ISBN: 979-8-3852-1418-1
EBOOK ISBN: 979-8-3852-1419-8

07/22/24

For my mother, Catherine McKittrick.
Your love and wisdom have shaped my life.
I love you.

.

Contents

Introduction

In the Daily Devotions with Jesus series, Rev. Dr. Graham Joseph Hill guides you through the entire Bible, moving from Genesis to Revelation. Daily Devotions with Jesus podcasts and devotional books show you how each book of the Bible can shape your spiritual life and actions in the world. This is a groundbreaking Bible podcast and devotional book series. See how each book of the Bible deepens your faith and inspires you to follow Jesus in life-changing ways!

The Gospel of Mark, the second book of the New Testament, serves as a profound narrative deeply enriching Christian spirituality. At its heart, Mark's Gospel is a vivid and concise account of Jesus's ministry, focusing primarily on his actions and miracles. This briskly paced narrative propels us into the core of Jesus's life, revealing him as the ultimate servant and the Son of God. Its simplicity and directness make it an accessible yet profoundly thought-provoking text for daily devotion and reflection.

One of the critical themes in Mark is the concept of the "Messianic Secret," where Jesus's identity and mission are gradually unveiled. This theme encourages believers to seek a deeper understanding and relationship with Jesus, moving beyond surface-level faith. The Gospel of Mark also emphasizes the importance of faith over sheer understanding, showing how trust in Jesus leads to spiritual insight and transformation.

The stories within Mark, from the calming of the storm to the feeding of the thousands, are not just historical accounts but are deeply symbolic, reflecting our spiritual journeys. They speak of hope, redemption, and the power of faith, inviting us to trust in God's provision and timing. The immediacy with which Mark presents the life of Jesus prompts us to consider the urgency of the gospel and our response to it.

As we study Mark's Gospel, we find teachings that extend and deepen our spiritual lives. It challenges us to follow Jesus more closely, surrender more fully, and live out our faith with boldness and compassion. In this way, Mark's Gospel isn't just an ancient text. It's a living, breathing guide, continually shaping and inspiring our daily walk with God.

Rooted in rigorous biblical and theological scholarship, this devotional encourages a fuller understanding of the Gospel of Mark and its relevance in today's world. Each day, readers are invited to meditate on a passage, reflecting on its overarching themes and intricate details. This holistic approach illuminates vital messages often overlooked in cursory or superficial readings.

This daily devotional doesn't shy away from biblical and theological depth. It makes no apology for pushing you to examine the theological and biblical meanings of the chapters you read. However, this exploration of Scripture isn't merely intellectual. It beckons the heart and spirit, urging readers to engage in intimate conversations with God, share the timeless message of the gospel, and be invigorated toward Christ-glorifying action. Drawing from the ancient narratives, readers will find inspiration to advocate for peace, champion justice, foster reconciliation, extend mercy, and actively partake in society's transformation.

Deep immersion in Scripture invariably leads to a more profound understanding of God's word and its implications for our lives. This devotional, rich with thought-provoking questions and guided prayers, catalyzes a deeper relationship with God. As you turn each page, may you be drawn closer to God's heart and spurred on to walk in the footsteps of Jesus. This is the fourth book in a series of devotional books designed to guide you through the entire Bible, nourishing your soul, renewing your purpose, and deepening your theology, contemplation, and action.

Here's what is inside this devotional and how best to use it:

1. The devotional covers the entire Gospel of Mark over fifty days.

2. Use this book with the Daily Devotions with Jesus podcast—https://grahamjosephhill.com/devotions.

3. Every day as you work your way through this devotional:

   a. *Read* the Bible passage slowly and prayerfully.

   b. *Listen* to the podcast episode for this Bible passage.

   c. *Reflect* on the spiritual devotional.

   d. *Pray* over the Bible passage and devotional and their meanings for your life and the world.

   e. *Act* on your insights.

Reading this Mark devotional alone, with family, or with a group will help you understand the Bible more fully and put it into practice. Get ready to change.

All Scripture quotations, unless otherwise indicated, are taken from the World English Bible.

Day 1

Humility and Readiness
for Our Messiah

Mark 1:1–8

The Gospel of Mark begins with John the Baptist appearing in the wilderness, preaching a baptism of repentance for the forgiveness of sins. John is a wild, untamed, radical, and prophetic figure, dressed in camel hair, eating locusts and wild honey, living in the wilderness, and calling people to get ready for the arrival of the Messiah. John doesn't live for himself. Instead, he is a voice calling in the wilderness, confronting people with the need to have clean hearts and prepare for the coming of the Messiah. John challenges his listeners to make the way for Jesus Christ by choosing repentance from sins, baptism into a new way of life, and cultivation of hearts that are ready and receptive to the Messiah whom the prophets foretold and who is soon coming.

John's message isn't about himself; it's about the coming Messiah, who is greater than John, who fulfills the prophecies of the Hebrew Scriptures, and who will baptize people with the Holy Spirit. In our narcissistic and media-saturated world, we are often tempted to make our lives the main story. Our accomplishments and egos take center stage in our social media posts, resumes, and storytelling. When we give into the spirit of this age, we fuel the focus on ego, pride, vanity, branding, narcissism, and self-promotion. Look at my achievements! See what I've done! Like and share my posts! Praise me for what difference I'm making in the world! We become the center of this story, and it doesn't glorify Jesus Christ.

The Messiah wants disciples who chose the path of humility. We are not the light; we are bearers of the light. Do our lives, thoughts, and words glorify and proclaim Jesus the Messiah? Is Jesus the heart of our social media posts, resumes, conversations, and stories? Do people leave our online or in-person presence feeling drawn to see Jesus Christ and him alone? We can't prepare the way for the Lord or make straight paths for him unless we embrace this humility. Being disciples means inviting Jesus Christ into our hearts, conversations, and lives so that these focus on Jesus, proclaim his good news, and draw people into a loving, saving relationship with him. As we prepare our hearts for Jesus, making room for God's love and grace, we bring our vulnerability, sinfulness, and longings to God, asking him to baptize us in the Holy Spirit, humble us so that we can truly glorify him, and make us messengers of faith, hope, and love.

Big Idea: A humble and repentant heart glorifies God and prepares the way for Jesus, his good news, extravagant grace, and love.

Reflection: Am I the center of my conversations, stories, and social media posts, or is Jesus the center? Are my choices building my reputation and future or are they aimed at glorifying and serving Jesus?

Prayer: Our Messiah, please give us humble, repentant, and soft hearts. Please help us make daily choices to set aside our ego and vanity and, instead, glorify you. May every part of our lives proclaim your good news. We bring our vulnerability and longings to you so that you might fill us and give us strength to be messengers of your gospel, preparing a way for you, our Lord and Savior. Amen.

Day 2

Jesus Is Vulnerable, Tested, and Fully Human

Mark 1:9–13

The parallels between John the Baptist and Jesus are striking. John is a voice crying out in the wilderness. Jesus goes silently into the wilderness after his baptism. John proclaims the coming of the Messiah. A voice from heaven declares Jesus is God's Son and beloved and hence is the Messiah. John baptizes with water. Jesus receives the Spirit as a dove while preparing to baptize his followers in the Holy Spirit. John's voice thunders in the wilderness. Jesus is confirmed as the Son of God, the promised Messiah, by a voice thundering from the heavens. John stands in the tradition of the Hebrew prophets and Scriptures, as does Jesus. Christ goes into the wilderness for forty days, symbolizing the journey of the Israelites, their purification and refinement, their dependence on God in the harshest of environments, and their preparation to fulfill God's will and plans.

So, while Jesus identifies with Israel and John the Baptist, it's also remarkable that he identifies with us in our humanity. No, it's more than that—it's astonishing. Jesus, the beloved of God, is fully immersed in the human condition from birth, throughout his life, and in Jordon's water and the desert's harsh terrain. Jesus

3

embraces our fears, our anxieties, our joys, our sufferings, and even our temptations. Jesus is fully God and completely human. We see and revere his divinity—as we should. But we must also strive to see his full humanity. Jesus completely identifies with us as we wrestle with temptations and grapple with desires, through our nights of turmoil due to our anxieties and fears, our suffering and pain, our confusion and anguish during periods of trauma, our boredom with the mundane, our fulfillment of our roles and responsibilities, and our periods of joy and celebration. Do you feel fear, sadness, anger, anxiety, love, amusement, frustration, compassion, pain, craving, or relief? Jesus felt all those things and fully entered our humanity.

When Jesus was baptized and spent time alone in the wilderness, he experienced the depth of God's love and intimacy. God descended on him in love and affirmation; God was with him in the wilderness, offering comfort, sustenance, and love. Even in moments of profound vulnerability and testing, we are not alone. Like God's comfort and presence with Jesus during his time of need, God is also with us in our trials and moments of desolation. God enters our experience, offering us love, hope, affirmation, and comfort. God gives us the presence of the Spirit, calling us into a deeper trust and a fuller relationship with the beloved.

Big Idea: Jesus fully identifies with our humanity. We are not alone, even during profound vulnerability, suffering, or testing. God is close and offers comfort and love.

Reflection: Do I believe Jesus fully enters my experiences and offers me love and comfort? What may be holding me back from accepting this fully?

Prayer: Loving God, please help us see your love and presence with us in all our experiences in life. Jesus's identification with us is a mystery. His journey with us in our pain, temptations, and joys is also difficult to fathom. But you are with us, comforting us with your presence, walking with us during times of vulnerability and testing, and offering us intimacy, hope, and love. Amen.

Day 3

Following Jesus and Announcing Good News

Mark 1:14-20

As Jesus announces the good news of the kingdom of God, he calls people to come and follow him. The good news Jesus proclaims is the good news he calls us to proclaim. The kingdom of God is where the sick are healed, the oppressed are set free, and the marginalized, silenced, despised,f and excluded are honored. The gospel isn't only for spiritual salvation; it touches every part of human experience, transforming the whole of people's lives, families, neighborhoods, and societies. Is our gospel holistic? Do we have a holistic vision of God's kingdom and its radical transformation of individual lives, the whole earth, and all aspects of society?

Jesus proclaims a kingdom where people return to God in repentance and discipleship. And this kingdom breaks into every dimension of our lives. The kingdom confronts social evils and ills and offers another way. This is a kingdom where everyone receives the health care they need without fearing whether they have the money to pay and where disciples take concrete actions to address poverty and economic inequalities built into our societies. This is a realm where students' debts are forgiven, wage inequality is eradicated, people have access to affordable and adequate health care, as well as affordable access to safe and affordable housing, and where we refuse to tolerate any forms of racism, sexism, ableism, classism, ageism, or religious discrimination. This is a kingdom where we take urgent action to address climate change and injustices, recognizing that the plight of the earth and the world's most vulnerable are intertwined. This is a realm where we take courageous action to address gun violence and where we refuse to allow political or financial interests to dictate the safety and well-being of our own children and the children of everyone in our society. Jesus proclaimed radical good news and called us as his disciples to follow him and do the same.

Following Jesus is joining a radical journey of transformation and service. Will we leave our nets behind and embrace Jesus's profound way of love, compassion, justice, and reconciliation? Are we willing to leave our comfort zones and follow Jesus as he builds a kingdom that confronts the powers, evils, injustices, brokenness, and systems of our culture and age? Will we learn the art of catching hearts, guided by the radical, untamed, wild message and gospel of our Messiah—a teacher who is also gentle and steadfast?

Big Idea: Jesus announces the transformative gospel of the kingdom and calls us to follow him by doing the same in word and action.

Reflection: Does my vision of the good news touch every aspect of life? Am I willing to set aside my pride, prejudices, interests, and privileges and follow Jesus, proclaiming his revolutionary gospel?

Prayer: Prophetic Messiah, give us the courage to follow you, laying aside our ideas, biases, and ways to proclaim the good news of the world-shattering kingdom of God. Amen.

Day 4

Following Our Compassionate, Praying Christ

Mark 1:21-45

As Jesus moves across Israel, he preaches the good news, drives out evil spirits, crosses social boundaries, heals people from their afflictions, teaches with authority, and prays in solitude. We see a divine dance between Jesus's compassion, prayer, inclusivity, boundary-crossing, teaching, and healing.

When we encounter people unlike us, it's easy to withhold our concern. But Jesus models a different way. Jesus is motivated by compassion as he moves among those rejected, excluded, and marginalized by society, religious leaders, and structures. He crosses boundaries with love, inclusion, and compassion. Jesus bends and breaks gender, ethnic, religious, social, political, and religious boundaries. Why? Because of a deep well of compassion and love. In our diverse and globalized world, we always rub shoulders with people different from us. Do we feel empathy? Are we moved with compassion? Can we have the courage to cross boundaries with love and inclusion? Are our hearts large, soft, and Christlike enough to embrace others with the healing power of inclusive, radical love and compassion? Do we follow the healing way of Jesus or the divisive, conflictual ways of so many voices in our world? Does our vision of the gospel and the kingdom of God move us with compassion and solidarity for all creation and humanity or make us cold and hard toward those who differ from us? Have we embraced the healing, liberating gospel of Jesus Christ, which makes our hearts compassionate, gentle, and kind? Or has a perverted version of the "gospel" seduced us and made our hearts reflect the divisions and exclusions fostered by the destructive principalities and powers of this age?

Where does Jesus find this compassion? What's the source of his desire and efforts to touch the untouchable, heal the despised, free the oppressed, cross social boundaries, and show astonishing compassion, dignity, and care to those society has shunned and excluded? In the early morning, while it's still dark, Jesus rises, goes to a solitary place, and prays. Jesus receives the compassion of God in solitude, on his knees in prayer. Prayer and solitude are transformative. Are you taking time for these? In our moments of solitude, let us listen for the gentle whisper of God's voice, guiding us back to our true home in Jesus Christ, empowered to serve with a heart full of compassion and love.

Big Idea: In times of prayer and solitude, God can fill our hearts with love and move us to compassionate action.

Reflection: How am I following Jesus's example to seek out those needing a healing touch? Am I regularly retreating for solitude and prayer, and how is this empowering me to serve others with God's love?

Prayer: Compassionate Healer, fill our hearts with a desire to touch the lives of those around us with your transformative love while nurturing our own, connecting with you in solitude and prayer. May we reach out to those society has cast aside, offering healing and dignity. May our compassion not be our own but an expression of your radical, incomparable love. Amen.

Day 5

The Power of Faith in Action

Mark 2:1–12

In the story of the paralytic healed by Jesus, we see the profound power of faith in action. We often think of faith as a solitary affair. We grit our teeth and are determined to believe. But when our faith falters, we realize that faith is rarely possible alone. Faith takes a community, especially one motivated by compassion and solidarity. The paralyzed man has faith, but that faith is upheld by the faith of those who love him. In this story, we see the astonishing power of faith in action, not just the faith of the one in need of healing but the collective faith of a community willing to dismantle roofs and overcome obstacles for the sake of one another. That's faith clothed in a community of love and sheer determination to ensure the well-being and healing of each other. Life bruises us, breaks us, wounds us, and hurts us. We all end up wounded in various ways, and all need a community of solidarity and love who show us compassion, uphold and bolster our faith, and carry us into the healing touch of our God.

This narrative invites us to consider the lengths to which we are called to go for the sake of love, to bring ourselves and our friends into the healing presence of Jesus. Will I expend my energy, time, resources, and reputation for the sake of others? Does the compassion of Christ move me? Has the love of God gripped my heart and moved me into compassionate action? Are we, in our communities and circles of friends, inspired to act with bold faith, tearing down the barriers that keep us from God and each other? When Jesus is called the "Son of God," people refer to his divinity. And when Jesus calls himself the "Son of Man," he's signifying his full humanity. Jesus shows compassion to all who come to him because, as the Son of God, he is clothed in God's divine, boundless compassion, and as the Son of Man, he fully identifies with our suffering, need, and frailty. Jesus has authority on earth to heal the broken and wounded, to receive our loving and compassionate faith in action, and to forgive sins. In our encounters with Jesus, we discover the healing we need and the freedom to walk in love and forgiveness. We only need to come to him and, in love, bring others to him, too.

Big Idea: Our shared, compassionate faith in action overcomes obstacles for healing, forgiveness, and spiritual connection and depends on the grace of Jesus Christ.

Reflection: How is Jesus's compassion moving me to faith in action? What steps can I take to join a community of disciples who practice collective faith and bring themselves and others to God?

Prayer: Lord Jesus, you heal us, welcome us, see us, identify with us, and forgive us. Please give us the compassion and strength to exercise faith in action, not merely as a solitary practice but as part of a forgiving and healing community. Amen.

Day 6

The Radical Inclusivity of Table Fellowship

Mark 2:13–17

Jesus calls Levi, a tax collector, to follow him and then dines with sinners and tax collectors, with the despised, marginalized, and lowest of society. This passage explores themes of inclusion, grace, and the radical invitation of Jesus to those on the margins.

Jesus's call to Levi and his shared table with tax collectors and sinners reminds us that God's love knows no bounds and excludes no one. When we eat with someone, we move toward empathy and intimacy, including them in our hearts and at our tables. There are few more intimate and inclusive acts than sharing a meal with others and few more radical acts than eating with those different from us or despised and rejected by society and religious people. This gesture of unconditional acceptance challenges us to look beyond societal labels and see the beloved child of God in each person.

Jesus regularly ate with the lowest and most despised of society and religion. He broke down social barriers, showed God's inclusive and radical love, and used these as teaching moments for his disciples. This practice, often called "table fellowship," served multiple theological and cultural purposes. In this radical table fellowship, Jesus challenged the prevailing social norms and barriers, offered a glimpse of the expansiveness and inclusiveness of the kingdom of God, and overturned notions of honor and status. Jesus showed God's unconditional love and mercy extended to all people, regardless of their standing in society, sinfulness, or any other condition that made them outcasts, despised, and rejected by society and religion.

Table fellowship remains a radical practice today. Our world is often characterized by social, economic, political, ethnic, and cultural divides. Sharing meals with people from different backgrounds, political leanings, religions, or social standings can be a powerful act of defiance against our age's polarized and antagonistic spirits. We can embody inclusion, empathy, and love. Sharing food offers spaces to bridge divides, challenge prejudices, promote equality, foster community, advocate for social justice, and renew inclusive and reconciling spirituality. "Blessed are the peacemakers, for they will be called children of God" (Matt 5:9). Blessed are those who love, dignify, and include sinners and the outcast and despised. They will be like Jesus, who "came not to call the righteous, but sinners" (Mark 2:17).

Big Idea: Table fellowship fosters inclusion, welcome, love, fellowship, and honor.

Reflection: Does Jesus's example move me? Will I extend invitations of fellowship, inclusion, and love to those whom the world and religions often overlook or reject? How can I embody the inclusive embrace of God's kingdom, where all are welcome and cherished?

Prayer: Gracious Jesus, give us the courage to follow your revolutionary example, opening our tables, homes, and lives to express divine inclusivity, love, acceptance, and forgiveness. May we have the courage to break down barriers and welcome all into a community of love and fellowship. Amen.

Day 7

New Wine for New Wineskins

Mark 2:18-28

Religiosity often differs from authentic spirituality and discipleship. We all need external expressions of faith, but when they become legalistic and controlling, they suffocate genuine faith, hope, and love.

Religiosity can often be about rules and conformity to external expectations. Authentic spirituality and discipleship are about an internal transformation, an inner change, and growth within our hearts, will, and minds, leading to actions that reflect the deeds of Jesus, done in the power of the Spirit. Religiosity can be superficial and external; authentic spirituality and discipleship is a deep, personal connection with the Divine. Religiosity can be focused on external pressures to conform to the rules and expectations of religious institutions and powers. Authentic spirituality and discipleship involve embodying our faith's ethical, moral, and compassionate values, expressed through acts of love and service, and concern for peace, righteousness, and justice. Religiosity can be cold and impersonal, treating humans as objects that need to serve institutions, rules, and rituals. Authentic spirituality and discipleship are warm and personal, and elevate and dignify the value of human beings, nurturing a personal relationship with God, others, and all creation. Religiosity can keep people immature; authentic spirituality and discipleship is a journey of continual growth, self-reflection, and seeking. The juxtapositions become clear: external versus internal, form versus essence, identity versus transformation, and conformity versus personal journey.

Religious traditions, rituals, and practices are valuable in spiritual life. But when they become "old wineskins and garments," controlling and dehumanizing people, they no longer serve their purpose or glorify God (vv. 21–22). To paraphrase Jesus, "Sabbath was made for human wellbeing, flourishing, and communing with God; humans weren't made to be controlled by the Sabbath. Jesus and his plans for humanity reign supreme over every religious institution and tradition" (vv. 27–28).

Jesus invites us to embrace the spirit of God's commandments, inviting us into a relationship with God that transcends legalistic observance. Jesus teaches us that the heart of our actions, our rituals, and our rest should not be bound by the constraints of tradition alone but filled with the liberating love of God that seeks our wholeness and well-being.

Big Idea: We should approach our practices and periods of rest with the question, "Does this bring me closer to the heart of God?"

Reflection: Does my life reflect the joyful freedom of loving attentiveness to God's presence in every moment? How do I practice rituals and traditions without them becoming controlling or mere external observances?

Prayer: Loving God, please draw us into a relationship with you that transcends legalistic observances. Teach us that the heart of our actions, rituals, and rest should not be bound by the constraints of tradition alone. Fill us with the liberating love of God that seeks our wholeness and well-being. Show us how to approach our practices and our periods of rest with a desire to draw closer to you and other people. May our lives be filled with joyful freedom in a loving, intimate, liberating relationship with you. Give us new wine for your new wineskins of faith, hope, and love. Amen.

Day 8

Choosing Compassion Over Legalism

Mark 3:1-6

Jesus chose compassion over legalism and love over rules. As Jesus moved through social and religious spaces, he wasn't interested in being a "religious or social influencer" by saying and doing the right things, sprouting religious or catchy slogans, eating and associating with the right people, appearing the right way, following rules that give the appearance of righteousness, or being controversial for the sake of attention. Instead, Jesus followed the will of the Father, showing compassion instead of self-righteousness and legalism, and lived a life that transcended a rigid adherence to rules and the need for acclaim, recognition, or applause. How does Jesus's example shape our lives?

Our temptation is to honor those the world honors, to strive to appear righteous, reach for religious and social influence, and cling to religious rules rather than compassion, inclusion, and love. Jesus shows us another way. In Mark 3:1–6, Jesus enters a synagogue and gravitates to a man with a shriveled hand. He draws near to those who are despised, outcasts, ridiculed, and of no importance in social and religious settings. Jesus reaches out to them with compassion, honoring and elevating them.

In this act of healing, Jesus reveals the heart of God's law is not constraint but compassion, not legalism but love. Jesus reaches out, honors, loves, and heals all who come to him, even you and me. In our greatest hour of need, Jesus offers compassion and hope. He truly sees us and loves us. Faced with human suffering, Jesus chooses to act, teaching us that faithful observance of God's commandments leads us to love more deeply and to see beyond the letter of the law to its spirit. When we follow the way of Jesus, we act in ways that are more fully human and more certainly humanizing. Instead of rules, we see people. Instead of acting with self-righteousness and judgmentalism, we serve with empathy and compassion. Instead of subjugating people to inflexible and harsh religious and social rules and laws, we see God's presence and image in everyone and especially seek to dignify and honor those who've been forgotten, silenced, and despised.

Big Idea: Jesus inspires us with his courage and compassion. Let's dare to lead lives that prioritize love and healing. Let's embrace the freedom to act with kindness, even when faced with misunderstanding or criticism, following the radical path of love that Jesus shows us.

Reflection: How can I follow Jesus's example and choose compassion over legalism and love over rules? Who are the ridiculed, despised, outcasts, or overlooked in our society whom I can love and serve? How do these marginalized people show me the heart of discipleship and the true person of Jesus Christ?

Prayer: Loving God, we depend on your courage to act compassionately. Help us see beyond rules to the heart of your love. Guard us from self-righteousness, self-promotion, and self-interestedness. Guide our hands to heal, our words to comfort, and our lives to reflect your grace. May we always choose love, embodying your presence in a world needing your healing and saving touch. Amen.

Day 9

Uniting Contemplation, Action, and Community

Mark 3:7-19

Amid crowds and miracles, Jesus withdraws to pray and selects the Twelve, reminding us of the rhythm of action and contemplation in our journey with God. There's a sacred dance in the spiritual life between contemplation and action, rest and effort, prayer and proclamation, meditation and work, and soul-searching and activism. True contemplation is a source of enormous energy in the world and a reservoir of vitality for Spirit-empowered action. Genuine contemplatives lead lives of meditation, prayer, and action—lives that refute the idea that contemplation is an escape from real life. Jesus withdrew from the crowds and service for regular silence, solitude, and prayer beside lakes, within deserts and gardens, and up into the mountains. If the Son of God needed solitude and prayer for revitalization and connection with the love of God and the power of the Spirit, how much more do we?

The disciples saw the dance between contemplation and action in Jesus's life, witnessing the enormous energy and determination Jesus received through meditation and solitude, and asked, "Lord, teach us to pray" (Luke 11:1). Jesus rose early in the morning for solitude and prayer, before conducting marvelous healings and

19

miracles (Mark 1:35). Jesus prayed frequently on mountains, including immediately before choosing the twelve apostles and during his transfiguration (Luke 6:12–13; 9:28–29). Jesus spent entire nights in prayer (Luke 6:12). In teaching the Lord's Prayer, Jesus provided a model of prayer that encompasses adoration, confession, thanksgiving, and supplication. We often miss that Jesus naturally weaves the Lord's Prayer into peacemaking, mercy, forgiveness, enemy love, fasting, and giving to the needy if we read the Sermon on the Mount. Jesus taught and modeled the intricate connection between prayer and action.

But contemplation and action also need community. Our prayers are often barren and actions fleeting and inadequate unless we're immersed in genuine community. Mark 3:7–19 speaks to our calling—to be chosen and sent out, not alone, but as part of a community of believers united in purpose and love.

Big Idea: The Spirit of God weaves contemplation, solitude, action, and community in our spiritual lives. Jesus intertwines these, nourishing our hearts, deepening our connection with God, energizing our discipleship and ministry, and uniting us in love and service.

Reflection: How will I set aside time to find strength and renewal in my solitude with God? Are my actions the overflow of contemplation? How can I embrace my role within the spiritual family, supporting and being supported, as I share God's love in the world?

Prayer: Lord Jesus, teach us to pray. Guide us into a life of contemplation and community so that your Spirit's power, joy, and vitality may energize our actions, ministries, and service. Amen.

Day 10

Remaining Steadfast When Facing Opposition

Mark 3:20–35

Throughout his life, Jesus faced opposition from religious, social, and political leaders, and even at times from family. Whenever we disrupt the status quo, ask and invite uncomfortable questions, or act in just, righteous, and loving ways, we can expect opposition and conflict. The principalities and powers don't like to be challenged. Social and religious norms often reflect deeply held values that contradict the freedom, holiness, grace, and love of God. Jesus told us to expect strife and opposition, encouraged us to remain steadfast in our faith, and offered us the comfort of the Holy Spirit.

When the power of Christ enters a situation, evil spirits resist—spirits of injustice, oppression, greed, lust, envy, pride, and more. And so, Jesus talks about his power and authority over demons. When God's kingdom breaks into the world, we see Jesus's power over darkness. Given the opposition we'll face from religious, social, and demonic forces, we must press into spiritual warfare, depending on prayer, faith, Scripture, and the name, power, and victory of Jesus Christ our Lord.

MARK

The other striking thing in this passage is the way Jesus
redefines family. We love our flesh and blood, as we should. But
Jesus says there's a kinship that goes deeper than blood relations—
spiritual family. Jesus unites us with other disciples who do the will
of God and makes us a new family. This family is shaped around
faith, obedience, and love, not ethnic or familial ties. We don't
always feel love among God's people. They hurt us and reject us.
They can act in ways that betray our confidence, trust, and sense
of safety. But this isn't the spiritual community Jesus envisioned.
Jesus spoke of a spiritual family committed to community and
belonging, which breaks down barriers and walls, and practices
radical inclusivity, welcome, and love. This family centers around
doing God's will.

What's the unforgivable sin? Verse 29 is difficult to interpret.
But it's probably harboring a hard and unbelieving heart that
refuses to recognize and attribute to God the works done by the
Holy Spirit through Jesus. The hard-hearted person looks at the
compassion, mercy, freedom, justice, and righteousness of Jesus
and refuses to acknowledge that this is the way and message of Jesus
and his kingdom. What's worse is that the hard-hearted person
says the ways of Christ are of the devil; therefore, blaspheming
against the Holy Spirit. It reminds us to cultivate soft, open hearts
to Jesus and his ways.

Big Idea: The kingdom of God contrasts with the kingdom of
Satan and the kingdoms of this world. We can join with Jesus in
dismantling the powers of evil and proclaiming the rule, reign, and
kingdom of God. This kingdom is marked by healing, liberation,
and spiritual family.

Reflection: How am I actively joining and participating in a
Christian spiritual community that will give me the strength to
resist social and spiritual opposition? How can I live out the values
of God's kingdom—justice, peace, love, and the undoing of evil
structures?

Prayer: Divine Creator, please strengthen us when facing opposition and conflict. Guide us to see beyond the barriers dividing us into a family united in your love. Please help us follow your will and embrace other disciples as our spiritual family. May our hearts be open, our actions kind, and our community a reflection of your radical, inclusive, world-transforming love. Help us remain steadfast when facing opposition, as your church and Spirit comfort us and give us strength, determination, love, and hope. Amen.

Day 11

Divine Seed and Human Soil

Mark 4:1-20

The parable of the sower speaks profoundly to our interior lives and the Spirit's call to profound, personal transformation through the intimate reception of God's word. The kingdom of God is like a seed sown in our hearts, revealing our receptivity to God's righteousness, regeneration, and reign. How will we respond? Will our hearts be hard, distracted, shallow, anxious, worldly, and barren? Or will our hearts be like the good soil, willing to repent and believe the good news of the kingdom of God, receptive to God's transforming love and grace, and fertile so that the seed produces abundance?

We must examine our hearts, considering how they receive and nurture the word of God. This introspection fosters a more fertile ground for spiritual growth and guards against complacency, shallowness, or distraction. Every day, we must prepare our hearts as fertile soil. As a gardener tenderly prepares the ground for sowing, we must cultivate silence, openness, repentance, obedience, and receptivity in our inner lives to truly hear and bear fruit from the Divine Word. This parable's emphasis on fruitfulness as an indicator of genuine faith challenges us to discern and cultivate spiritual fruits in our lives—love, joy, peace, patience, and others—as evidence of a deep, transformative relationship with God. Am I tending the soil of my heart?

We needn't lose hope when we find our hearts shallow, hard, complacent, or distracted. The Spirit of Christ isn't finished with us. God has the final word. Jesus can turn our hard paths, rocky places, and thorny ground into good, receptive, fertile soil. We don't manufacture good soil or produce a crop in our effort. We depend on God's power, presence, and grace, given to us through our Lord Jesus Christ. This truth reminds us of the paradox of vulnerability and strength in spiritual growth. Acknowledging our weaknesses and distractions—our rocky, thorny, and hard paths— can lead to a deeper dependence on God's grace, transforming us into rich soil that nurtures a bountiful harvest of love, joy, and peace in our lives and the lives of those around us.

Big Idea: The Spirit of Christ invites us to surrender our hearts' soil to the Divine Sower. God can cause our weaknesses and vulnerabilities to bloom into a harvest of strength and love, revealing the kingdom of God within us. Our role is to prepare our hearts to be receptive.

Reflection: What kind of soil is my heart? How am I tending the soil of my heart? Am I choosing to let God turn my rocky, thorny, and hard paths into good soil?

Prayer: Jesus Christ, the living Word of God, please take deep root in our hearts, transforming us from within. As we open ourselves to your divine sowing, we recognize our vulnerabilities not as barriers but as gateways to grace and transformation. We invite the seed of your endless love to sprout within us. May we embody the paradoxical mystery of the kingdom of God: that in our deepest weakness lies our greatest strength, and in our surrender, our most profound flourishing. Amen.

Day 12

Mustard Seeds and Strong, Large Trees

Mark 4:21–34

We live in an individualistic and performative age. Contemporary Western societies are capitalistic, materialistic, consumeristic, performance-oriented, and individualistic, exporting these values globally. What does this culture value? Work hard. Depend on yourself. Make plans and strategies. Pull yourself up by your bootstraps. Focus on yourself. Wealth, achievements, and possessions measure success. Your happiness is paramount. Performance and productivity define your worth. Individual achievement trumps community and well-being. Self-reliance and independence are critical. Visibility and recognition matter. All growth and change should be noticeable and exponential. Happiness and fulfillment can be bought.

These verses contrast such modern messages. Jesus describes the gentle yet transformative power of the kingdom of God and the need for us to rest and trust in God's work while responding faithfully to that process. What does Jesus say is essential in the kingdom of God? God's kingdom values integrity and intrinsic worth over material wealth, status, and possessions. Growth and value come from what's hidden and unseen. God's timing and manner of growth are paramount. Significance starts with small beginnings. Begin with the mustard seed of God's kingdom—love, integrity, faithfulness, righteousness, justice, the fruits of the Spirit, and so on—and see God's Spirit nurture these into solid and large trees that provide shade for all who seek shelter. Depend on God rather than being self-reliant. Be known and seen by God, rather than striving for the social status of human acknowledgment. Joy and fulfillment come from spiritual growth.

Our daily lives are sacred, the fertile soil where the smallest seeds of faith are sown. This seed, nurtured in the hiddenness of our hearts, promises a harvest beyond our comprehension. Like the lamp not meant to be hidden, our lives are to shine in the darkness, revealing God's love through acts of kindness, patience, and mercy. We don't need to be anxious about our lives. Growth, change, and significance are mysterious and in God's hands; our role is to live with integrity, receptivity, and faithfulness. While we sleep and rise, God works in the depths of our being, transforming our small efforts into signs of God's kingdom.

Big Idea: We can trust God's slow, often unseen work. Our smallest acts of faith contribute to the grand, unfolding story of God's love in the world.

Reflection: Does culture shape my actions and values, or is the kingdom of God transforming them? How can I find space to rest and trust in God, knowing he's doing something with the mustard seeds in my life?

Prayer: Loving God, in the loving and gentle whispers of your Spirit and Word, plant your kingdom's seeds in our heart's hidden gardens. Please help us value the ways of your kingdom instead of being drawn into the concerns of this world. Nurture our souls with your tender care, that we may grow in love, bear fruit in darkness, and offer shelter to those seeking refuge in your unfailing grace. Amen.

Day 13

God's Love and Presence
amid the Storm

Mark 4:35-41

On the voyage of life, we often encounter many storms. Many of these are unexpected. They can terrify us and threaten to swamp the boats of our lives and our sense of safety, worth, dignity, and security. Many of us find ourselves crying out to Jesus, "Teacher, don't you care if we drown?" Jesus wants us to hear his loving, comforting voice, "Don't be afraid, I'm here with you, I love you, I'll care for you, so have faith and don't be afraid."

I've experienced more loss, pain, and grief in my life than I ever imagined possible. The love of friends and family has been my comfort. This love mirrors Christ's comfort, calling me to trust instead of fear and to have faith instead of doubt, anxiety, and despair.

For many people, the storms of life are grief and loss. Grief plays havoc with your heart, mind, and body, and when we grieve, we realize we mustn't take loved ones for granted. Grief comes in waves, and you feel it deep in your heart and your body's core. You feel you must move forward but don't have to move on. Life is worth living, but the joy and solace are in the simple, little things you may have once missed. Memories can comfort but also wound and hurt more profoundly than you imagined. Grief and guilt are companions, often inviting shame to the table. These things frequently coexist—grief and hope, faith and doubt, trust and fear. When you lose a dream or person you care deeply about, you feel like you've lost part of yourself. Grief is like someone turned up the dial on our memories, guilt, anger, fears, anxieties, panic, sadness, yearning, and more. It's difficult to concentrate, and you feel confused, often moving between intense feelings and a state of being numb. When you're in a storm, you ask, "When will this pain end?" "Teacher, don't you care if I drown?"

Everyone's experience of loss and grief is personal and unique. These are just my experiences. But I've found solace in the love of others and hope that coexists with grief. Grief and loss have given me a deeper compassion and love for the broken and a fuller pastoral heart. I've also found a clearer sense of call in ministry and a more profound love for people and family. This growth has been a surprise and shows the grace of God. Maybe this is the loving, often unseen, gentle work of the kingdom mentioned elsewhere in Mark 4, which can grow from a seed into a tree. Jesus comes to us in the storm and says, "I'm holding, loving, supporting, and guiding you. Don't be afraid. Let my love nurture and produce your faith." True peace comes not from the absence of trouble but from the assurance of Christ's presence with us in every moment, encouraging us to surrender our fears and trust in the One who calms the sea.

Big Idea: Our boats are often rocked by waves of fear, grief, loss, doubt, and turmoil. Jesus is always present, asking us, "Why are you so afraid? I love you, I'm present with you, and I'll care for you. Have you still no faith?"

Reflection: How are you responding to God's invitation to deeper faith and trust in his presence and care, even when he seems silent or distant? How is God calling you to surrender your fears and trust his love and comfort amid the storm?

Prayer: Gentle Jesus, be our calm amid life's storms. When fears rise like waves and doubt darkens our sky, help our hearts experience your peace. Remind us of your nearness, that in knowing you are with us, we find the courage to trust, and in your presence, our fears dissolve. Amen.

Day 14

From Chains to Jesus's Healing and Freeing Love

Mark 5:1-20

The story of the restoration of the demon-possessed man tells of a person who was both feared and broken, terrifying and rejected, violent and enslaved. This account is a striking image of a man in bondage to evil forces, driven by spirits to live among the tombs and break restraining chains, cut himself with sharp stones, and cry out in agony from the graveyards and hills. This is a heartbreaking narrative about a man rejected and feared by society, shunned and despised by neighbors, living on the margins and without hope. Jesus doesn't only see the evil forces that oppress him. Jesus sees his lonely, enslaved, broken heart and his longing for love, inclusion, freedom, and hope. Jesus doesn't only free him from the evil spirits but restores him to community. This man encounters the love and embrace of God, the healing and freeing power of the Son of God, and the hope and liberation only Jesus can offer. Jesus restores him to his neighbors and community, giving him the message of the kingdom of God, a message of hope, freedom, and the power and love of the Messiah.

The healing love and power of Jesus can profoundly transform us. The story of the Gerasene demoniac shows Jesus's power not only to heal our deepest wounds but also to free us from the chains that bind us—be they addiction, despair, isolation, or fear. This story calls us to recognize the areas of our lives where we need Jesus's liberating touch and to trust in Christ's compassionate desire to restore us to the fullness of life. Jesus heals this man physically, socially, and spiritually. The healing love, power, and embrace of Jesus can heal every aspect of our lives, freeing us from the darkest forces that bind us. When we open ourselves to Jesus's liberating touch, we open ourselves to freedom, hope, community, confidence, and courage. Jesus replaces bondage with freedom, exclusion with inclusion, and despair with faith, hope, and love.

Notice the man's response to Jesus's healing—an eagerness to follow Christ. This response teaches us about the nature of discipleship as a journey from brokenness to wholeness, from isolation to community, and from despair to hope.

Big Idea: Jesus's love can replace the spirits that enslave us and the chains that bind us with freedom, wholeness, relationship, and hope.

Reflection: What areas of my life need Jesus's liberating touch? Am I trusting Christ's compassionate power to restore, heal, and free me?

Prayer: Compassionate Healer, in our brokenness, you meet us with mercy. Cast out the shadows that lurk within and free us from the chains that bind our spirits. Help us to trust your compassionate power and presence. May your love restore us so we can walk in the light of your freedom, proclaiming your healing grace in every word and deed. Amen.

Day 15

Healing and Lifegiving Touch, Words, and Actions

Mark 5:21–43

There's healing power in touch. In one of these stories, a woman reaches out and touches Jesus and is healed. In the other, Jesus touches a child who has died and raises her to life. Touch communicates and transmits profound things between people. Our touch can offer hope for those who are hopeless, love for those who feel alone, comfort for those who mourn, freedom for those who suffer, and life for those who have died on the inside.

The stories in Mark 5:21–43 are primarily about the compassion and power of Jesus the Messiah, which are evidence that he is the Son of God. Everyone he touches feels his power and messianic nature, experiences his compassion and love, and is drawn into a space where love, inclusion, healing, and life are offered. Human touch is powerful but a dim reflection of the touch of Jesus Christ. But, when Christ has touched us, and his love and compassion have healed, liberated, and brought us back to life, our touch is transformed. Our touch brings the healing, comfort, and new life of God. Our touch can say, "God and I love you. God has seen your faith and struggles and loves you with a love that's eternal and unconditional. Go in peace and be freed from your suffering. Understandably, you're fearful and anxious, but don't be afraid; only believe. You are loved. You are included. You are a person of deep value and worth. The love of God can bring you back to life, hope, healing, and divine and human connection."

The heart of compassion is at the core of Jesus's touch and divine actions. Jesus teaches us to be fully present to one another in our brokenness, desires, sufferings, and hopes. The woman's courage in this story is astonishing as she reaches out to touch Jesus in faith. The desperation of Jairus is palpable as he, a respected leader, humbles himself to plead for his daughter's life. In these actions, we see God's call to vulnerability—a willingness to expose our wounds and lay bare our needs before God and each other.

Jesus's healing words and touch restore us to community—not just the cessation of physical ailments but the invitation back into full life and relationship. In Jesus, we find someone who crosses all boundaries to reach us, offering himself as a source of healing and resurrection. Our journeys of faith require us to reach out, even in fear or doubt, to touch and be touched by the Divine, believing in the transformative power of God's love to bring life even in the most desperate circumstances. This is where our true healing lies—not just for ourselves but in our ability to bring this healing presence into the lives of those around us, embodying Jesus's compassion and care.

Big Idea: Jesus offers healing, lifegiving words and touch, and guides us to do the same.

Reflection: Am I seeking and open to Jesus's healing touch? How can I offer healing words and touch to others? Does my heart reflect the compassion at the core of Jesus's touch and divine actions?

Prayer: Healing Messiah, please touch us with your love and healing power. We need your comfort and hope. May we have the courage of the woman who reached out and touched Jesus and the faith of Jairus, who believed that Jesus offers healing and can bring us back from the dead. May we provide a healing touch and loving embrace to others so that they would experience God's healing, life-giving, and resurrection power. Amen.

Day 16

Allegiance to the Prophet without Honor

Mark 6:1-6

Jesus was a prophet without honor. Nothing about his behavior and words made sense to those looking for a victorious Messiah or a virtuous spiritual leader. Jesus's humility, compassion, and servanthood contrasted the ways of the Jewish, Greek, and Roman political and religious leaders and continue to contrast such leaders today.

The church and world don't need any more forceful, charismatic, opinionated, egotistical leaders. These usually create environments of fear and pain, rather than healing, love, hope, and renewal. More than ever, we need leadership characterized by humility, self-sacrifice, wisdom, integrity, and love. We need godly, humble, holy leaders more than gifted leaders with charisma. The church and society need leaders who serve in the imitation of Christ and in the way of the cross.

When we serve this way, we can expect persecution and dishonor. If Jesus suffered and was dishonored, why would we expect anything different? But that's what happens when we pledge allegiance to the servant King, the suffering Messiah, the prophet without honor. Can you say these words? "I pledge allegiance to the revolutionary peasant King, who suffered at the hands of the religious and powerful, who bled and died on a shameful hill outside the gates and beyond the walls, who was tortured and imprisoned and murdered and forgotten, who received the death penalty for blasphemy and treason, and who God rose gloriously from the dead. I pledge allegiance to his gospel of salvation and his eternal kingdom—a kingdom that replaces violence with peace, strength with weakness, pride with humility, force with submission, control with vulnerability, autonomy with intimacy, accumulation with simplicity, exclusion with welcome, exploitation with justice, greed with generosity, ambition with contentment, bigotry with equality, indifference with compassion, punishment with mercy, judgment with forgiveness, imprisonment with freedom, and fear with love. I pledge allegiance to Jesus Christ and his just, merciful, righteous, and peaceable kingdom."

Jesus revealed the paradox of strength found in our willingness to be vulnerable, misunderstood, and even dismissed by those closest to us. Jesus was undeterred by disbelief and skepticism. He embraced his vulnerability, revealing the deep, often painful, path to authentic ministry. We may be dishonored along the way, but this is the path of the Messiah, our glorified peasant King.

Big Idea: Strive to embody the humility, compassion, and servant-hearted nature of Jesus, contrasting the prevalent societal norms of forceful and self-serving leadership. Prepare to embrace vulnerability and possible dishonor while pursuing authentic, Christlike service.

Reflection: How can I follow Jesus and embrace his humility and compassion more faithfully this week, even if it leads to dishonor or rejection by those around me? What and to whom am I pledging allegiance? What changes in my lifestyle and values would be necessary if I pledged allegiance to Jesus?

Prayer: Divine Teacher, in your footsteps, we seek the quiet strength of humility and the courage to serve, not to be served.

Help us to embody your compassion and love, facing scorn with the grace you showed. Mold our hearts to mirror yours, leading by serving in your peaceable kingdom. Please help us to follow you and imitate your actions as you empower us with your Holy Spirit. Amen.

Day 17

Embracing Radical Trust

Mark 6:7-13

When Jesus sent out the Twelve, he didn't just give them a mission, he transformed their lives. He instructed them to take nothing for the journey but a staff—no bread, no bag, no money in their belts. This was a stark contrast to the security they were used to. This passage speaks profoundly about trust and dependence on God, as Jesus invites his disciples into a vulnerability that requires them to rely not on their provisions but on the hospitality and goodness of those they meet. Do we trust God in this way? Are we willing to be vulnerable and receive the hospitality of those we meet as we serve Jesus? Some will accept and welcome us. Others will reject, dishonor, or even persecute us. This reality draws us into a more profound trust and dependence on God.

As modern-day disciples, Jesus calls us too into this radical trust. Jesus teaches us that the mission of sharing God's love necessitates simplicity and poverty of spirit. It challenges us to let go of our securities and comforts, to step out in faith with the essentials, trusting that God will provide through the communities we serve. This stripping away is physical and spiritual, where we surrender our desire for control and open ourselves to God's unexpected provisions. The mission of the disciples was profound—leaving their security and comfort to travel and spread the good news of the kingdom of God, taking very little with them, entering homes and receiving hospitality, preaching the message of Jesus, calling people to repentance, driving out evil and impure spirits, and healing the sick. And Jesus instructs them to do all this in a spirit of trust and dependence on God's power, presence, and provision. This life of radical trust and dependence on God brings joy and fulfillment beyond measure.

Jesus's instruction to stay in one place until they leave suggests a call to stability and presence. We are invited not to flit from one place to another but to deeply engage with the people and places we are sent to, forming relationships and building community. Like the disciples, Jesus may call us to leave our homes and comfort zones to spread the kingdom's good news. Yet, Jesus always calls us to go where we can build genuine relationships based on mutuality and love. These relationships are not just a by-product of our service, but are the very essence and impact of it.

Big Idea: Jesus teaches us to embrace radical trust and dependence on God. The Spirit of Christ invites us into a vulnerable faith that relies on divine provision and the hospitality of others.

Reflection: In what areas of my life do I find it challenging to rely solely on God's provision? How can I practice vulnerability and openness in receiving hospitality and support from others in my community?

Prayer: Lord Jesus, please give us the courage to embrace simplicity and trust. You know our weaknesses and desires, yet you love us immensely and are always with us. May we learn to depend more fully on God, finding in our vulnerability a deeper freedom and joy in our mission to spread your love. Please guide us on this journey of discipleship and mission. Teach us that this is not merely an outward journey but an inward journey toward greater faith and reliance on your Holy Spirit and our loving God, who calls and sends us forth. Amen.

Day 18

Speaking Truth to Power

Mark 6:14-29

In Mark 6:14-29, we are confronted with the poignant tale of John the Baptist's martyrdom—a narrative that vividly portrays the bravery and sacrifice of prophetic witness and the intricate dance of power, fear, and truth. John's unwavering courage in upholding truth, despite the threat of imprisonment and death, raises profound questions about our call to speak truth to power.

As disciples of Christ, we are entrusted with the duty of truth, often necessitating us to stand against prevailing currents of deception or injustice. John's uncompromising integrity in confronting Herod about his unlawful marriage is a powerful reminder that truth-telling is an essential aspect of discipleship and a responsibility. It prompts us to reflect: How often do we silence our voices, dilute our messages, or look the other way to maintain our safety or status?

What might speaking truth to power look like today? Speaking with courage means standing against the dehumanizing, destructive forces of this world and standing up for the well-being of all people, among all racial, religious, and other groups, at all stages of life. Speaking truth to power involves standing up for the flourishing and well-being of all human and ecological life, with a vision shaped by the shalom of the gospel and Christ's kingdom.

This "prophetic" way includes doing our small part in a community to address our modern age's injustices, exploitations, and sins. What might speaking truth to power include? Opposing unjust and cruel immigration detention policies and practices. Upholding the rights of all minorities and religious groups. Caring for the rights and well-being of asylum seekers and refugees. Addressing global warming, environmental destruction, and climate change. Healing political and religious tensions. Honoring Indigenous and First Nations peoples and their voices, claims, and rights. Refusing the way of war, conflict, and violence. Finding fresh ways to address rising nationalism and antagonism between groups. Caring about poverty and the inequality between rich and poor—a society is only as just and good as the way it treats its poorest and most vulnerable citizens. Speaking up about economic and political corruption. Healing racial, ethnic, and ideological tensions and refusing to fan them into flame. Supporting initiatives that address pornography and an alarming sexualization of culture. Addressing modern slavery and human trafficking. Caring for those families and communities suffering from drought, flood, fire, and other disasters. Making sure all people have access to the education and health care they need. Finding creative ways to support those who are addicted and confronting the institutions that encourage addiction (drugs, gambling, alcohol, pornography, and so on). Helping to build a society that deals honestly with gender, class, and racial injustices.

Most of us can only do small things, and all things are best done in and through community. Let's embrace a bigger vision of what it means to speak truth to power in the traditions of the prophets and our Lord Jesus. This prophetic vision got John the Baptist killed, and we don't know how we will suffer. But our passion is shaped by the vision of the gospel of Christ and the shalom of God.

Big Idea: We can draw courage from John the Baptist, praying for the strength to live authentically and boldly while speaking truth to power.

Reflection: How might Jesus be calling me to speak truth to power? Where can I find the support and encouragement to do so? What issues would Jesus and the prophets have addressed today, and what would they have said?

Prayer: God of truth and justice, please help us hold fast to truth, trusting in your ultimate justice and mercy, even when faced with the world's resistance. May we honor John's legacy and fulfill our calling as bearers of light in a shadowed world. In the light of John the Baptist's unwavering courage, please encourage us to embrace the prophetic call of our discipleship. Grant us the strength to speak truth in the face of deception and power and to stand firm in justice and love. Nurture in us a spirit not of fear, but of power, love, and self-discipline. May we honor your truth in every word we speak and in every action we take, guided by the radiant light of Christ. Please help us to support each other in this journey, finding courage through community to transform our world in the vision of your peace. Amen.

Day 19

Embracing the Scandal of Compassion

Mark 6:30-44

As Jesus mixed with the crowds and among those suffering from poverty, exclusion, and social and religious stigma and abandonment, he always offered compassion and kindness. Followers of Jesus are compassionate, gentle, and kind—living testimonies to the grace and love of God. When Jesus fed the five thousand, he showed his characteristic compassion for humanity, which would take him to the cross.

There are few things more scandalous than the cross of Jesus Christ. In Christ crucified, God reveals compassion, power, love, and wisdom. Jesus defies human wisdom and strength and shows a God who suffers and bleeds. God chooses vulnerability and suffering and honors the lowly and foolish things of this world to shame the strong and the wise. Ridiculous, outrageous, bizarre. In so doing, Jesus is our righteousness, holiness, wisdom, strength, and redemption.

The scandalous church follows the way of the cross, soaked in compassion, leading lives worthy of the gospel. We replace cruelty with kindness, fear with love, ego with humility, aggression with tenderness, prejudice with compassion, control with service, strength with vulnerability, and a grasping after life with a willingness to suffer and die. Weak and foolish by the world's standards, we choose to bless not curse, to persevere under suffering, and to answer our accusers and slanderers with kindness. "We are made as the filth of the world, the dirt wiped off by all, even until now" (1 Cor 4:13). We are foolish and weak gluttons and drunkards, but the wisdom and power of God is "justified by all her children" (Luke 7:33–35). But we are also the people of the resurrection! "'Death is swallowed up in victory' . . . But thanks be to God, who gives us the victory through our Lord Jesus Christ" (1 Cor 15:54–57).

The compassion of Christ is shocking and scandalous. When we conform to the image of Jesus Christ, we do not conform to the world's cruelty, violence, injustice, antagonisms, falsehoods, and indifference. A conformed church confronts injustice, heals divisions, rejects hypocrisy, shows mercy, welcomes strangers, fellowships with sinners, and offers compassion to all. Our compassion is weird, our holiness is offensive, our peace is reconciling, and our lifestyles are questionable.

In feeding the five thousand, we see another example of how Jesus always coupled his proclamation of the gospel with works of healing, justice, and compassion. Our compassion, social justice, and gospel proclamation are inseparable. In all this, we seek to reject prejudice, pride, power, and control; instead, we embrace humility and weakness. We are holy fools. We are simultaneously all sinners and all saints, and we welcome all people everywhere to God's banquet table. We live strange, dangerous, compassionate, and prophetic lives as we cling to the wisdom, power, and scandal of Christ crucified and resurrected.

Big Idea: The feeding of the five thousand exemplifies the radical, scandalous nature of Jesus's compassion. Followers of Jesus must embody a transformative, countercultural compassion that defies worldly wisdom and embraces vulnerability, mirroring Christ's path to the cross and resurrection.

Reflection: In what ways might you be called to embody Christ's scandalous compassion in your daily interactions and choices? How can you actively challenge societal norms and values contradicting the teachings of humility, vulnerability, and love demonstrated by Jesus?

Prayer: Gracious God, infuse our hearts with Christ's scandalous compassion. Empower us to embrace humility, suffer with the oppressed, and love unconditionally. May our lives reflect the radical, transformative grace that challenges, heals, and renews. Let us live as witnesses to your ultimate victory of love. Amen.

Day 20

Finding Peace in the Storm

Mark 6:45–56

After the miraculous event of the loaves and fishes, Jesus, sensing the need for solitude, withdraws to the mountains to pray, leaving his disciples to navigate the sea. Isolated in their boat, they confront the darkness and the intensifying storm. Fear engulfs them as the wind rages and the waves pummel their fragile vessel. In these moments of extreme danger, they are alone, yet not forsaken.

Amidst the chaos, Jesus approaches them, walking on water, a profound display of the Divine breaking through human fears. Yet, even in their terror, they fail to identify him, confusing him for a specter. How frequently do we, too, overlook the divine intervention in our turbulent times, blinded by our anxieties?

Jesus speaks, "Take courage! It is I. Don't be afraid" (v. 50, NIV). His voice is a call for bravery and a gentle reminder of his unending presence. In the moments of our greatest despair, Jesus is closest, walking beside us, even on the tumultuous seas of our lives.

As Jesus steps into the boat with the disciples, the storm subsides. Isn't this the ultimate comfort? With Christ among them, tranquility is restored. The tempests of hardship may not vanish instantly, but in his presence, there is a peace that surpasses all comprehension.

This passage invites us to recognize Christ in our midst, especially in the storms. It calls us to trust deeper, reminding us that fear dissipates when faith takes its place. Let's open our hearts to the tranquility of knowing Jesus is always near, whispering through our storms, "It's me; don't be afraid."

When Jesus and the disciples land at Gennesaret, people run to him from throughout the whole region. Wherever Jesus went—in the villages, towns, and countrywide—people brought their sick to him, placing them where he might touch and heal them. And when Jesus does touch people, they are healed. Again, people bring their physical illnesses to Christ and their fears, alienations, and traumas, and he heals them. Just like the story of Jesus walking on the water and calming the storm, Jesus meets people where they are and brings healing, peace, and divine reassurance that God is with us even during the storms or wounds of life.

Big Idea: Amid life's storms, recognizing Jesus's presence brings healing, dispels fear, and restores peace.

Reflection: How does it feel to know that Jesus is beside you even amid the storms of life and is ready to heal you from all your hurts and wounds? What chaos, fear, anxiety, hurt, or trauma will you bring to Jesus today, seeking peace and healing?

Prayer: Loving God, we seek your calming and healing presence amid our storms. As the waves rise and the winds roar, remind us that you are with us, walking on water, calming the sea. Help us recognize you even in the chaos and hear your voice saying, "Don't be afraid." Grant us the courage to trust in you, to let go of our fears, and to embrace the peace only you can provide. May we hold firm in faith, knowing you are always near, our constant guide and protector. Heal us from all our illnesses and wounds, whether in our body or spirit. In your loving name, we pray. Amen.

Day 21

Pure Hearts beyond Rituals

Mark 7:1–23

In Mark 7, we encounter a profound teaching moment between Jesus and the Pharisees centered around the heart's true purity. With their deep commitment to tradition, the Pharisees question Jesus about his disciples' disregard for ceremonial handwashing. Jesus responds by addressing the hypocrisy of the religious leaders. Quoting the prophet Isaiah, Jesus says it's possible to honor God with our words but have hearts far removed from God's ways. It's also a problem when we worship God in vain through practices soaked in human rituals, rules, and needlessly weighty obligations. These don't lead to God's freedom, justice, or love and burden people in ways God never intended. But notice that Jesus doesn't condemn the crowds—he calls them to deeper introspection, challenging the superficial rituals that have overshadowed the essence of their faith.

We're not defiled by what we eat and drink but by what comes out of our hearts in our actions and words. With these words, Jesus shifts our focus from external practices to the internal source: our heart. Jesus invites us to ponder on the origin of our actions and thoughts. This is a profound reminder that our spirituality is not measured by our external adherence to rituals and religious practices but by the purity of our hearts.

This passage presents us with a challenge—to align our external practices with our inner commitment. Are our actions driven by love, compassion, and justice? Or do they stem from unexamined places of greed, prejudice, and malice? Do our words and actions align with God's righteousness and justice? Or do they produce the fruit of evil thoughts? Jesus calls these "evils" and includes "adulteries, sexual sins, murders, thefts, covetings, wickedness, deceit, lustful desires, an evil eye, blasphemy, pride, and foolishness. All these evil things come from within, and defile the man" (vv. 21–23). The challenge is ensuring that our external practices reflect our inner commitment to love God and our neighbor.

In our spiritual journey, let's keep sight of what truly matters. Let's cleanse our hearts, making them wellsprings of God's love and truth. May our daily rituals always remind us of our deeper call to live out the love of Christ, showing the world the beauty of a heart truly aligned with God's will. This is the path to genuine purity, a journey that begins and ends in the heart.

Big Idea: True spiritual purity flows from the heart, transcending external rituals.

Reflection: Are my daily practices expressions of a heart aligned with God's truth and healing love for the world? Do my words and actions reflect a heart cultivated by compassion and justice when I experience stress or disagreement? Or are there traces of unresolved bitterness and judgment?

Prayer: Gracious God, guide our hearts towards true purity so that our actions and words may reflect your deep love and justice. May our words and actions reflect your beauty and righteousness, showing people your desire to draw them into your forgiveness, healing, and embrace. Please help us discern and cleanse the inner places that hinder our walk with you. Amen.

Day 22

Faith beyond Boundaries

Mark 7:24-30

In the encounter between Jesus and the Syrophoenician woman in Mark 7:24-30, we find a profound lesson on faith, humility, and the expansive mercy of God. Jesus, seeking respite in the region of Tyre, enters a house, hoping not to be disturbed. Yet, even here, Jesus's presence draws those in desperate need. Jesus may want to keep his presence secret, but people tell of his love, teachings, and spiritual power, and seek him out wherever he goes.

The woman who approaches Jesus embodies both desperation and determination. She suffers great anxiety over her daughter's plight, and she's a person of tremendous faith and courage. Imagine the shame and social exclusion she has experienced! Imagine the courage it must have taken to seek out and approach Jesus for help. An evil spirit torments her daughter, and she believes that Jesus can heal her. She is a Gentile, not a Jew, and thus stands outside the traditional boundaries of those Jesus has come to serve. Her approach breaks through these boundaries, driven by a mother's love and fueled by a faith that societal divisions will not deter.

Jesus's initial response to her plea might startle us, as he speaks of not taking the children's bread and throwing it to the dogs. It seems harsh but within his words is a test of faith and perhaps a deeper lesson for his disciples about the reach of God's kingdom. Maybe he's even parodying the perspectives of the Jews and the religious leaders of the time to show the woman and his disciples that the kingdom of God is more inclusive and expansive than they'd imagined. The woman's reply, marked by humility and sharp wit, "Even the dogs under the table eat the children's crumbs" (v. 28), reveals a profound understanding of grace that knows no bounds. While Jesus's words are harsh and reflect the religious views of many Jews, the woman sees with eyes of faith—eyes that see the compassion, generosity, and inclusivity of Jesus and the kingdom of God. Even the crumbs of the kingdom of God have tremendous power to heal and draw all people into God's family and redemption. Jesus once again sees incredible faith shown in the most unexpected places.

This moment is transformative. Jesus acknowledges her faith, saying, "For this saying, go your way. The demon has gone out of your daughter " (v. 29). Her faith and persistence draw a blessing from Jesus that transcends cultural and religious barriers.

This story invites us to reflect on our understanding of faith and inclusivity. Are there boundaries we have constructed within our hearts that limit our understanding of who deserves God's mercy? The faith of the Syrophoenician woman teaches us that God's love is not confined by the boundaries we draw.

Big Idea: The Syrophoenician woman's encounter with Jesus teaches us that faith and God's mercy transcend cultural and religious boundaries. God calls us to reflect the faith of the Syrophoenician woman and the compassion and mercy of Jesus Christ.

Reflection: When will I take time today to pray for faith as bold and persistent as that of the Syrophoenician woman? What's hindering me from believing in the boundlessness of God's mercy? Am I learning to see beyond human-made boundaries and welcome all who seek God's grace?

Prayer: Lord, grant us a boundless faith that sees beyond borders and believes deeply in your expansive grace. Help us embrace others with the compassion shown by Jesus Christ, drawing near to all who seek your healing love. Amen.

Day 23

Opening to Divine Restoration

Mark 7:31-37

Jesus meets us in our weaknesses and struggles with compassion and healing. Jesus comes to us when our hearts and lives are broken and says, "Ephphatha," which means "Be opened," but which also communicates, "You are loved, you are seen, you are valued, and I will heal you."

In the story of Jesus's healing of a deaf and mute man, we witness a tender moment of healing and revelation. Jesus, traveling through the region of Decapolis, encounters a man who is deaf and has an impediment in his speech. The people bring him to Jesus, imploring that he might touch him. In this gesture of bringing the man to Jesus, we see the beautiful interplay of community and divine intervention. This story is about many things: friendship and longing, community and desire, human brokenness and divine love, and much more.

Jesus takes the man aside in privacy, away from the crowd. This act of secluding him reflects a deep respect for the man's dignity. It's a personal encounter where healing is not just a public spectacle but an intimate act of restoration. Jesus then uses elements of the earth—his fingers and saliva—emphasizing his connection to humanity and his role as the Creator who reforms and restores. Jesus touches him, and this touch communicates the presence and love of God. Jesus constantly reaches out to people who are desperate and touches them, sharing the embrace of a God who sees their hearts, hears their prayers, touches their humanity, includes them in God's family, and heals their pain.

Jesus looks to heaven, sighs, and commands, "Be opened!" (v. 34). At this moment, the barriers of the man's physical limitations are broken, his ears are opened, his tongue is released, and he speaks plainly. This physical opening is also a spiritual revelation. It signifies the opening of a deeper understanding among the people of who Jesus is—the healer, the Messiah, and the one who reconciles us to God and one another.

Jesus commands them to tell no one, yet the more he orders them, the more zealously they proclaim it. Their overwhelming response, "He has done all things well" (v. 37), reveals a recognition of Jesus's messianic identity, his love for humanity, and his restoration of creation.

This narrative calls us to consider our own areas of isolation and impairment. Where do we need Jesus to say, "Be opened"? It may not be our ears or our mouth but perhaps our hearts, minds, or eyes. Like the community in Decapolis, we are not just invited, but entrusted with the task of bringing ourselves and others to Jesus, believing in his restoring touch. The Spirit of Christ invites us to pray for the openness to hear Jesus's voice and the courage to speak his truths. In our interactions, may we reflect the compassion and respect Jesus shows, and may we too be instruments of his healing and love in the world.

Big Idea: Jesus's healing touch is not just a physical act but a transformative power that opens us to deeper spiritual understanding and connection.

Reflection: In what areas of your life are you seeking healing or understanding? How can you more openly invite Jesus into these spaces to work his restorative power? Reflect on your role within your community: How can you help bring others to experience the transformative touch of compassion and grace, just as the people brought the deaf man to Jesus?

Prayer: Loving Savior, gently open our hearts, ears, and mouths to fully receive and proclaim your truth. Help us embody your healing presence, bringing light and love to those hidden in the shadows of isolation. You see and touch us. Guide us to be a similar healing presence in other people's lives. Amen.

Day 24

Faith in the Desert

Mark 8:1-13

In many stories in the four Gospels, we're struck by the compassion of Jesus. When people present their needs, Jesus responds with love and mercy, and we see Christ's compassionate heart again in the feeding of the four thousand. As Jesus observes the crowds and their needs, he feels compassion, noticing they are hungry and far from home. He turns to his disciples, revealing the depth of his concern, yet they respond with confusion: "How can one feed these people with bread here in the desert? How would we get enough bread for these crowds in this remote place?"

This passage invites us to consider our deserts—those barren stretches in our lives where hope seems sparse and sustenance scarce. We see the needs around us and feel overwhelmed. Often, we find ourselves echoing the disciples' question, unsure of how our meager resources could possibly meet the vast needs before us. Yet, the heart of the message here is not about the scarcity but about the transformative power of faith. It's about how our small offerings, when made in faith, can catalyze divine abundance, turning our deserts into fertile grounds of hope and provision.

Jesus asks his disciples what he asks of us: to bring whatever we have, however insufficient it seems. In the divine economy, our small offerings are enough to begin a miracle. The loaves and fishes, so few against so many, become a feast that satisfies all. This miracle is not just about the multiplication of food but about the transformation of the heart. Will we respond with compassion that reflects the heart of God?

When we face hungry crowds—whether they hunger for bread, love, or justice—we are called not to be paralyzed by our perceived inadequacies but to offer what we have with a whole heart. It is in this offering that we find the true miracle: not only is the physical hunger of the people met, but our own spiritual hunger is satisfied. We discover the joy of giving, the joy of serving, and the joy of being part of a divine plan. In giving, we receive, and in serving, we are served.

As we reflect on this story, it's critical that we also choose not to be like the Pharisees who demand a sign but fail to perceive the miracles already unfolding before them. Instead, may we embrace the everyday miracles of compassion and provision, trusting that what we offer in love will always be enough.

Big Idea: In our spiritual deserts, even our smallest offerings, made in faith, can catalyze divine abundance.

Reflection: In what ways am I experiencing a "desert" in my life, and how can I offer my small resources to God's service within it? How does trusting in God's provision challenge or change my response to feeling inadequate?

Prayer: Loving Father, in the vastness of our needs and the simplicity of our offerings, teach us to trust in your abundant provision. Please help us see beyond our scarcity to the richness of your mercy. In moments of doubt, fortify our hearts with the courage to give what little we have. May our humble contributions become seeds of your boundless grace, blossoming into a harvest of hope and sustenance for ourselves and those around us. As we navigate our deserts, keep our eyes fixed on you, the source of all nourishment and peace. Amen.

Day 25

Discerning Subtle Influences

Mark 8:14-21

As the disciples sail with Jesus across the lake, he issues a crucial warning, "Take heed: beware of the yeast of the Pharisees and the yeast of Herod" (v. 15). This caution, often overlooked, carries profound implications for our spiritual journey. Yet, the disciples, consumed by the scarcity of bread, fail to grasp the essence of Jesus's message.

This moment starkly contrasts the disciples' fixation on the immediate and material—having only one loaf of bread—against Jesus's invitation to a deeper, more profound awareness. It prompts us to consider how often we, like the disciples, are consumed by the tangible "bread" in our lives—our daily needs and problems—and overlook the transformative teachings that life presents us with.

Jesus's repeated questions to his disciples are a poignant reminder of the patience required in our spiritual journey. They prompt us to recall and reflect on the countless times we have witnessed miracles and yet, in our human frailty, continue to doubt or fail to comprehend the vastness of God's presence and goodness in our lives.

In our modern lives, the "yeast "can be pervasive influences that subtly yet profoundly shape our perceptions and behaviors.

These influences might be societal pressures that prioritize material success over spiritual depth or cynicism that erodes our hope and faith. The "yeast "may also be the rules and regulations of religious systems, which keep us from the freedom and joy of Jesus Christ.

This passage invites us to deeper reflection, to look beyond our immediate concerns, and to understand the true nature of Christ's gifts and wisdom. It challenges us to ask ourselves how the subtle influences in our lives shape our actions and thoughts and whether we are genuinely heeding the spiritual nourishment that Christ offers over the fleeting satisfaction of earthly concerns.

Big Idea: Beyond our immediate concerns, we must discern and resist the subtle influences that distract us from deeper spiritual truths.

Reflection: What daily "yeast" might be fermenting unnoticed in my spiritual life, subtly shaping my beliefs and actions? How can I cultivate greater awareness and understanding of the deeper messages that God is communicating to me amidst my daily concerns?

Prayer: Gracious God, guide us to discern the subtle influences that shape our lives more than we realize. Please help us see beyond our immediate needs and fears to the deeper truths you wish to teach us. As we face our daily challenges, infuse us with the wisdom to recognize your guidance and the strength to resist the distractions that lead us away from you. May our hearts be tuned to your voice and our lives reflect your deeper will. Teach us to trust in your providential care and to engage with the world through the lens of your eternal love. Amen.

Day 26

Stages of Spiritual Clarity

Mark 8:22-26

In the passage of Mark 8:22-26, we encounter the profound moment where Jesus heals a blind man at Bethsaida. The man is brought to Jesus, who leads him out of the village, away from the crowd, into a quiet place. Jesus places saliva on the man's eyes and asks if he can see. The man's response is illuminating—he sees people, but they look like trees walking around. Jesus touches his eyes again and the man's sight is fully restored; he sees everything clearly.

The journey of the blind man in this story mirrors our own spiritual journey. When Jesus first touches his eyes, his vision is only partially restored. This mirrors our initial understandings, our glimpses of truth, which often come to us not all at once, but in stages. Our first insights into spiritual realities might be unclear or distorted, like seeing men as "trees walking" (v. 24). Yet, Jesus does not leave the man in his halfway state. With another touch, clarity is achieved.

This gradual healing process resonates deeply with our experiences of spiritual growth. Often, our understanding of God and God's ways are incremental. We receive grace in layers, insight upon insight, allowing us to move progressively closer to seeing things as they truly are. Through the illuminating and healing touch of Jesus, we see God, reality, humanity, and creation clearly. Our eyes and hearts are opened to see God's image in people, concern for justice and reconciliation, compassion for creation and those in need, and immense love.

This passage underscores the importance of patience and persistence in our spiritual lives. It urges us not to settle for partial understanding or incomplete vision. Instead, it beckons us to trust in the ongoing work of divine touch in our lives, which guides us from partial sight to full clarity, from dim perception to bright understanding.

How should we respond? Let's go into life with humility, understanding that our vision can always become clearer, our insights deeper, and our understanding more complete. Let's stay receptive to the continuing transformative touch of grace that leads us into fuller light and sharper vision of God's presence, grace, and love in our lives.

Big Idea: Our spiritual understanding unfolds gradually, requiring patience and openness to the incremental touches of divine grace.

Reflection: In what areas of my life am I experiencing only partial sight, and how can I remain open to further healing? How does gradually deepening my understanding of spiritual truths influence my faith and actions?

Prayer: Loving God, in the quiet moments of our encounter, touch our eyes so that we might see more clearly. Please help us understand that our journey with you unfolds in stages, each touch bringing us closer to complete clarity. Grant us patience as we navigate the dimly lit paths and faith to trust that you are with us, refining our sight and deepening our understanding. As we progress in our spiritual journey, keep our hearts open to your transformative grace so that we may fully embrace the vision you have for us. May we cherish each step that brings us closer to seeing the world through your eyes. Amen.

Day 27

Embracing Divine Wisdom

Mark 8:27-33

In this story, we encounter a pivotal moment in the disciples' journey with Jesus. As they walk towards the villages around Caesarea Philippi, Jesus asks, "Who do men say that I am?" (v. 27). After hearing their responses, he directs this question inward, "But who do you say that I am?" Peter answers, "You are the Christ" (v. 29). This acknowledgment marks a deepening in understanding, yet the path forward remains fraught with misunderstanding as Jesus begins to teach them about the suffering that awaits him, which Peter rebukes.

This passage invites us to reflect on the nature of our spiritual journey. Like Peter, it is not uncommon to find ourselves at a crossroads of spiritual insight and personal challenge. We might recognize Jesus as the Lord in one moment, only to resist his teachings when they threaten our expectations or understanding of how our journey should unfold.

Jesus's rebuke of Peter, "Get behind me, Satan! For you have in mind not the things of God, but the things of men" (v. 33), is a stark reminder of the tension between divine wisdom and human desires. This moment in Scripture challenges us to consider where we set our minds and hearts. Are we open to the divine, even when it calls us into pathways of suffering and sacrifice that we would rather avoid?

This narrative also deepens our understanding of discipleship. To truly follow Jesus means setting aside our agendas and embracing the journey of transformation, even when it leads through paths of pain and sacrifice. It calls us to a discipleship of not only recognizing Jesus with our lips but also following him with our lives, especially when his way diverges sharply from our expectations.

As we contemplate this passage, let's ask ourselves where we are being called to let go of our desires to truly embrace the way of the cross, trusting that through this surrender, we find the path to true life.

Big Idea: True discipleship requires embracing divine wisdom, even when it challenges our deepest expectations and desires.

Reflection: Where am I resisting Jesus's teachings because they do not align with my expectations or desires? How can I cultivate a heart open to divine guidance, especially when it leads through difficult or unexpected paths?

Prayer: Gracious God, in the unfolding journey with you, teach us to trust in your divine wisdom even when it leads us through valleys of uncertainty and sacrifice. Please help us acknowledge you with our words and follow you with our entire being. Strengthen our faith when we are tempted to choose easier paths that conform to our desires. Grant us the courage to let go of our expectations and to embrace your way, the way of the cross that leads to true and everlasting life. May our hearts always align with your divine will as we seek to become true disciples in thought, word, and deed. Amen.

Day 28

Embracing the Cross

Mark 8:34-9:1

Jesus shows us the way of the cross and discipleship: "Whoever wants to come after me, let him deny himself, and take up his cross, and follow me" (v. 34). This invitation to self-denial and cross bearing is an invitation to a profound and transformative journey that reshapes the essence of our being.

This passage invites us into a radical form of selflessness that is not about self-destruction but about discovering our true selves in the light of divine love. It challenges us to look beyond our immediate desires and fears to a deeper understanding of who we are meant to be. Taking up our cross is not merely an acceptance of suffering but an embrace of a way of life that prioritizes love, sacrifice, and humility.

The call to "lose one's life" for Jesus and the gospel is a paradox that reveals a profound truth: in giving up our grip on earthly life, we gain eternal life. It is in the giving we receive; it is in the dying to self that we are born to eternal life. This divine paradox is the heart of the Christian journey, where true freedom and joy are found not in accumulation and achievement but in surrender and service.

As we reflect on this passage, let's consider what crosses we are called to bear. They're often where we find our deepest connection to others and God. These crosses, these burdens, become sacred opportunities for transformation and love.

When we confront the fear of being "ashamed" of Christ, we face our deep-seated fears of vulnerability and rejection. These fears challenge us to question our adherence to societal norms over divine truths. Embracing Jesus's radical message offers us a pathway to overcome these fears through the transformative power of God's love. Let us live unashamed, rooted in our identity as beloved, and discover a deeper fulfillment in expressing the eternal through our daily lives, embodying courage and authenticity in every action.

Let's approach this divine invitation with courage and hope, trusting that the path of self-denial leads to the fullness of life. May we embrace our crosses, knowing that in them lies our true calling and deepest joy, as we follow in Christ's footsteps.

Big Idea: True freedom and joy are discovered not through self-preservation but through self-giving in the pattern of Christ.

Reflection: What does "taking up my cross" mean in my daily life and relationships? How might surrendering my desires for control lead to deeper freedom and joy?

Prayer: Lord, guide us as we strive to follow the path you have laid out for us, a path marked by self-denial and deep love. Please help us to embrace our crosses, not as burdens, but as gateways to discovering our true selves in you. Grant us the courage to let go of our ego-driven desires so that we may live more fully for others and you. May we find ourselves in each act of self-giving to be a step closer to the eternal joy and peace you promise. Teach us to lose our lives for your sake so that in doing so, we might find them anew in your boundless grace. Amen.

Day 29

Revelation on the Mountain

Mark 9:2–13

The transfiguration of Jesus is an event of profound mystery and illumination. Jesus leads Peter, James, and John up a high mountain, where they see him transfigured before them, his clothes dazzling white. Accompanied by Elijah and Moses, this vision transcends time and space, revealing the profound continuity between the law, the prophets, and Jesus's life.

This mountaintop experience is a moment of intimate disclosure, where the divine glory of Jesus is unveiled to his closest disciples. It is a foretaste of the resurrection, a promise of what is to come, and yet, it is also deeply rooted in the reality of Jesus's journey towards the cross. The voice from the cloud, saying, "This is my beloved Son. Listen to him" (v. 7), invites the disciples and us into a deeper obedience and attentiveness to Jesus's words and way. The loving relationship between the Father and the Son is also evident and a reminder that all profound relationships, including those that are divine, are formed by love, mutuality, and commitment.

However, as they descend the mountain, Jesus charges them to keep the vision secret until the Son of Man has risen from the dead, adding complexity and anticipation to their experience. They grapple with what "rising from the dead" could mean, revealing their incomplete understanding and the gradual unfolding of divine revelation.

This narrative invites us to reflect on the moments of clarity and revelation in our spiritual journeys. Like the disciples, we may not fully understand these experiences in the moment. They are glimpses that do not always come with immediate clarity but invite us into deeper reflection and engagement with the mysteries of faith.

As those loved by God, let's hold these moments of spiritual transfiguration with reverence and humility, allowing them to guide us more deeply into the way of Christ. They are gifts that prepare us for the challenges ahead, rooting our journey not just in the reality of human suffering but in the promise of divine glory. Thus, we are called to listen deeply and follow faithfully, bearing the light of these mountaintop moments into the everyday pathways of our lives.

Big Idea: Mountaintop moments of revelation invite us to deeper faith and understanding, preparing us for life's valleys.

Reflection: How do I integrate the revelations of my "mountaintop" experiences into my daily life and challenges? What does "listening to him" mean in the context of my own spiritual journey and daily decisions?

Prayer: Gracious God, you reveal your glory on the mountaintops and valleys of our lives. Please help us to cherish these moments of profound insight and carry their light into our everyday paths. Grant us the faith to trust your guidance, even when the vision fades and the path becomes unclear. Teach us to listen deeply to your voice so that we may follow you more faithfully and live out the truths you have shown us. Your love and presence are with us in every experience of life. We can rest and trust in you. Amen.

Day 30

Faith amid Doubt

Mark 9:14-29

In the story of Jesus healing a boy possessed by an impure spirit, we encounter the profound human experience of doubt juxtaposed with divine possibility. As Jesus descends from the Mount of Transfiguration, he is thrust into the midst of turmoil—a crowd disputing around his disciples, who are unable to heal a boy possessed by a spirit. The boy's father pleads with Jesus, voicing his mixture of hope and despair: "If you can do anything, have compassion on us, and help us" (v. 22).

Jesus's response in verse 23, "If you can believe, all things are possible to him who believes," is a powerful call to faith amid the realities of our struggles and doubts. The father's heartfelt cry, "I believe. Help my unbelief!" (v. 24) echoes the duality of human experience—our capacity to hold belief and unbelief simultaneously. This declaration is not a statement of failure but a profound acknowledgment of his need for divine assistance to bridge the gap between human limitation and divine power. How often have you struggled with the tension between belief and unbelief and the push and pull between faith and doubt? That's a human experience. Jesus understands this struggle, has compassion, and meets our needs.

This story is a deep well of spiritual reflection, revealing that faith is not a static state but a dynamic and ongoing journey of trust and transformation. It invites us to bring our doubts and struggles to Jesus, trusting in his ability to work within and through them. It also challenges us to confront the "unbelief" within us—not with judgment but with a humble request for help that comes from a heart aware of its limitations. Jesus is always compassionate and merciful, willing to meet us in our pain, doubt, and unbelief. While others may judge us for wrestling with doubt, Jesus never does. Instead, he meets us where we are and offers us love and access to his divine faith.

As we reflect on this narrative, we're invited to consider our places of "unbelief"—the areas of our lives where we find it hard to see God's hand at work. How do we respond to Jesus's invitation to believe in the face of seemingly insurmountable challenges? Like the boy's father, we can approach God with an honest acknowledgment of our doubts and a sincere plea for the faith we need. In this sacred space of vulnerability, our faith is deepened and our spirits are transformed, opening the way for God to do the impossible in and through us.

Big Idea: Jesus meets us in our doubts and unbelief and offers us love and his faith, transforming our struggles into a bridge toward divine possibilities.

Reflection: Where do I find the tension between belief and unbelief most pronounced in my spiritual life? How can I openly bring my doubts to God as part of my journey toward deeper faith?

Prayer: Loving God, when our hearts waver between belief and unbelief, we cry to you for help. Strengthen our faith even as we confront our doubts. May our honest struggles open us to the miraculous workings of your spirit. Please help us trust in your boundless compassion and power, even when overwhelmed by the challenges before us. Let our faith grow not despite our doubts but through them as we learn to rely more fully on your grace and love. Thank you for meeting us in our struggles and offering us your compassion, love, and divine faith. Lord, we believe. Please help us in our unbelief. Amen.

Day 31

Greatness in Humility

Mark 9:30-37

In Mark 9:30–37, we find Jesus imparting one of his most profound teachings to the disciples, centered on humility and service. As they travel through Galilee, Jesus teaches them privately, emphasizing that the Son of Man is to be delivered into human hands. Yet, the disciples struggle with this message, their minds entangled in worldly notions of power and prestige.

This dissonance becomes evident when Jesus, aware of their conversation about who among them is the greatest, presents a child as a symbol of true greatness in the kingdom of God. Jesus reverses the worldly metrics of importance and power by placing the child in their midst. He teaches, "Whoever receives one such little child in my name, receives me, and whoever receives me, doesn't receive me, but him who sent me" (v. 37).

This scene invites us to deeply self-reflect on our understanding of greatness and service. In our world, where status and power often dictate value, Jesus presents a radical alternative: true greatness comes through servanthood and humility. Welcoming the "little ones"—those who are dependent, overlooked, or undervalued—is welcoming God.

This message challenges us to consider who the "little ones" are in our lives. How are we called to serve and welcome them? The act of welcoming does not merely refer to physical reception but to a deep, heartfelt recognition and valuing of others, especially those marginalized by society.

Recent—and ancient—high-profile leadership failings show us that leadership idols, myths, and dysfunctions are seriously damaging the church and its witness. These include narcissism and pride and the desire for (and pursuit of) status, brand, power, control, popularity, and success.

It's time for our servant-ministers to adopt a different posture and language among us and within the world—one patterned after Jesus Christ. I'm still reflecting on what this looks like, but it seems to me that it must be a way of life (discipleship) shaped around these ten things:

1. Love (including loving service)

2. Faith (formed in trust and dependency)

3. Humility (including relinquishing brand, status, and control)

4. Integrity (in every aspect of life)

5. Prayer (as the heart of service and ministry)

6. Collaboration (giving yourself truly to community)

7. Grace (including honoring others and embracing simplicity)

8. Discipleship (as our primary vocation and call)

9. Vulnerability (weakness, transparency, and honesty)

10. Hope (putting your legacy and efforts into a different frame).

As followers of Christ, we are called to embody this radical hospitality and humility, recognizing that we serve Christ in serving the least among us. Let us strive to see the face of Jesus in all we encounter, particularly the "little ones," and let our lives be shaped by the grace of service rather than the pursuit of greatness.

Big Idea: True greatness in God's kingdom is measured by our humility and service to the least among us.

Reflection: How can I cultivate a spirit of humility in my daily interactions and relationships? Who are the "little ones" in my community, and how am I called to welcome and serve them?

Prayer: Gracious God, teach us the path of humility that your Son modeled for us. Open our hearts to recognize and embrace those often overlooked or undervalued. Please help us find true greatness in the quiet acts of service and the welcoming of the least among us. May our lives reflect your love and hospitality, drawing others to your compassionate embrace. Instill in us a spirit of humility that sees and serves Christ in every person we meet. Through our actions, may we proclaim the upside-down values of your kingdom, where the last become first and the first last. Amen.

Day 32

Radical Discipleship's Call

Mark 9:38-50

We are often tempted to exclude people different from us and include those we know. Our instinct is to welcome some and reject others, often for relational, ideological, or arbitrary reasons. In a world addicted to exclusion, prejudice, hostility, and conflict, choosing compassion and inclusion are radical and nonconformist acts that protest the way things currently are.

This passage begins with the disciples encountering someone casting out demons in Jesus's name, although he is not part of their immediate group. Their initial response is to stop him, but Jesus corrects them, saying, "Don't forbid him . . . For whoever is not against us is on our side" (v. 39). This response invites us to a broader understanding of community and collaboration, where we recognize and celebrate the work of God in diverse places and people. God's grace and presence are among those we least expect, often working powerfully in and through them.

Jesus then shifts the focus to the responsibilities of those in his community. He speaks of the severe consequences for those who lead these "little ones"—those new or vulnerable in faith—astray. Here, the call to integrity in discipleship is palpable. Jesus uses vivid language about cutting off hands or feet or plucking out eyes if they cause us to sin. This hyperbolic speech underscores the serious commitment required to follow him and foster a community that truly reflects his love and holiness. We must care for those who are vulnerable and live with character and integrity.

The final verses speak to being "salted with fire" and the importance of salt as a metaphor for the preservative and enhancing qualities that disciples are to bring to the world. Yet, Jesus warns that salt can lose its saltiness, leading us to consider how we maintain the essence of our spiritual vitality.

This passage calls us to self-examination and radical discipleship. It asks us to consider how inclusive our understanding of God's work in the world is and challenges us to live in ways that genuinely preserve and enhance the faith community. How do we react to God's work done in ways or by people unfamiliar to us? Are we maintaining the purity and commitment of our faith in a way that supports and does not hinder others? As we reflect on these questions, let us seek to embody the inclusive, preserving, and sanctifying presence that Jesus calls us to be in the world.

Big Idea: True discipleship beckons us to embody an inclusive and transformative presence that nurtures and safeguards the community's spiritual vigor.

Reflection: How do I cultivate an openness to witness and value God's workings, even when manifested through unfamiliar or unconventional ministries? Who has God included that I've excluded? What specific aspects of my life might I need to "cut off" or transform to not only preserve my faith but also to actively enhance the spiritual life of my community?

Prayer: Lord of all, you call us to a discipleship that transcends boundaries and challenges our comforts. Inspire us to recognize the divine in paths not our own and to cherish your presence in varied expressions of faith. Instill in us a courageous commitment to remove any barriers within ourselves that obstruct the flow of your grace. May we be agents of your salt and light, preserving the essence of our faith while promoting a faithful and flourishing community. Help us live out this radical call with integrity and love, reflecting your inclusive and life-giving spirit. Amen.

Day 33

Sacredness of Relationships

Mark 10:1-12

In this passage, Jesus offers profound teaching on the complex issues of marriage and divorce. The Pharisees approached him, seeking to test his understanding of the law, asking, "Is it lawful for a man to divorce his wife?" (v. 1). Jesus responds not by simply interpreting the law but by revealing the deeper intentions of the heart that the law seeks to guide. Once again, Jesus shows that a rigid interpretation of biblical passages can miss the compassion, holiness, and love of God. God's covenantal love sets the stage not merely for God's relationship with us but also our relationships with each other.

Jesus reminds the Pharisees of the creation story, where man and woman were made for each other, united so deeply that they become "one flesh." This original unity is not merely a legal bond but a profound sacramental union reflecting the relational nature of God. Jesus then emphasizes that what God has joined together, no one should separate. After all, this is how God approaches covenants.

This teaching invites us to reflect on the depth of commitment and the sanctity of relationships. It challenges us to view our relationships not just as legal or social agreements but as sacred covenants that mirror divine love. In a world where relationships can often be seen as temporary or disposable based on individual fulfillment, Jesus calls us to remember the deeper spiritual dimension that every authentic love relationship is meant to reflect.

Furthermore, this passage calls us to a broader reflection on all our relationships. How do we honor the sacredness of our connections with others? Are we nurturing unity and fidelity that reflect God's unending love for us?

As we ponder these questions, let us seek the grace to live out our relationships in a manner that brings life and reflects the divine. In our interactions, may we embody the compassion, fidelity, and commitment that Jesus teaches us, recognizing that in each genuine encounter, we touch the sacred, participating in the divine unity and love God desires for all humanity.

In light of this passage, we must also extend a tender hand to those for whom marriage has been marked by pain and brokenness. For those who have walked through the valley of divorce, the church must be a place of compassion and healing, not judgment. The heart of God is close to the brokenhearted, and God's grace is sufficient for all, regardless of our past. In the embrace of the Christian community, may you find a refuge where wounds are tended to with the balm of grace and understanding. The healing journey is long and often difficult, but you should not walk alone. There is a love that covers, heals, and redeems even the deepest of scars, and it is this love that we, as a community, are called to embody.

Big Idea: Our relationships are sacred covenants that reflect God's divine unity and enduring love.

Reflection: How can I more fully recognize and honor the divine dimension in my relationships, seeing them as sacred spaces of mutual growth and love? How might I deepen my commitment to embody fidelity and compassion, reflecting God's unconditional love in my interactions with others?

Prayer: Gracious God, you made all humanity and creation in relationship and called it good. Please help us to treasure the profound unity intended in our relationships. Teach us to see our bonds with others not merely as ties of convenience or habit but as sacred commitments that mirror your love. In moments of difficulty and decision, guide us to act with integrity and compassion, always striving to maintain the unity you desire. May our relationships be spaces of mutual respect, deep affection, and enduring commitment so that your love is manifest in the world through them. Amen.

Day 34

Heart of a Child

Mark 10:13-16

Jesus's interaction with little children captures the essence of the kingdom of God. The disciples, perhaps seeing the children as trivial distractions, initially rebuke those bringing the children to Jesus. But Jesus, discerning deeper truths, welcomes them with a profound proclamation: "Allow the little children to come to me! Don't forbid them, for God's Kingdom belongs to such as these" (v. 14).

Jesus offers a spiritual lesson on the nature of receptivity and humility. He uses the example of children, who, in their simplicity, vulnerability, and trust, embody the posture that we are all called to assume in our spiritual journey. Children do not rely on their power or understanding; their approach to life is marked by openness and a profound trust in those who care for them.

In an age where we are taught to be independent, ambitious, and self-assured, Jesus says the kingdom of God belongs to those who recognize their need, embrace their vulnerability, trust in God's care, and display humility and receptivity. Jesus's declaration that the kingdom of God belongs to such as these invites us to reflect on our approach to faith and life. Do we come to God and one another with the same openness and trust? Or are our hearts guarded, weighed down by cynicism, pride, or the illusion of self-sufficiency?

Jesus's blessing of the children points to the sacredness of blessing each life we encounter. Every person, regardless of age or status, holds a cherished place in God's heart and should thus be treated with tenderness and respect. Disciples of Jesus are marked by the respect they show for all persons and creation, regardless of race, religion, politics, or any other matter. We bless, honor, and embrace all people because Jesus does.

As we ponder this passage, let's seek to cultivate a heart like a child's—open to wonder, trust, and joy. Let's also remember our call to welcome and bless others, recognizing each person's inherent dignity and worth as a reflection of the divine. In embracing this childlike openness and respect for all, we draw nearer to the heart of the kingdom of God.

Big Idea: Embracing a childlike heart that is open and trusting unlocks the true essence of God's kingdom.

Reflection: How can I cultivate a more childlike trust and openness in my relationship with God and others? In what ways might my actions or attitudes hinder the "little children"—the pure and simple in spirit—from coming to Jesus?

Prayer: Dear Lord, guide us to embrace the humility and simplicity of a child. Help us to trust wholly in your love and to approach each day with a heart unburdened by pride or pretense. Teach us to receive and offer blessings with the innocent joy of a child, recognizing the sacredness in ourselves and in each person we meet. May our lives reflect the openness, delight, and trust you cherish in the little children so that we might genuinely enter and embody the kingdom of God. Let us always remember the grace of seeing the world through eyes filled with wonder and hearts full of faith. Amen.

Day 35

Freedom in Letting Go

Mark 10:17-31

In Mark 10, we encounter a poignant narrative of encounter and challenge. A man runs up to Jesus, kneels before him, and asks what he must do to inherit eternal life. Jesus, perceiving the depth of his yearning yet also the attachments binding his soul, provides an answer that transcends simple moral instruction. Jesus invites the man to sell all he has, give to people experiencing poverty, and follow him. This is a call to radical discipleship that ultimately proves too great for the man, as he leaves in sorrow, unable to relinquish his possessions.

This story is a profound meditation on the nature of true wealth and the cost of discipleship. It exposes the tension between our earthly entanglements and our spiritual aspirations. The man desires eternal life, yet his material wealth acts as a barrier, revealing how our possessions can consume us and prevent us from fully embracing the life to which Jesus calls us. At the time in history when Jesus talked about the difficulties the rich had in entering his kingdom, he was speaking about a small percentage of the population. Today, when we consider the relative wealth of the middle classes, Jesus is talking about me, possibly you, and a large percentage of the church and world.

Jesus's response to the man's departure is equally telling. He explains to his disciples how hard it is for the rich to enter the kingdom of God, likening it to a camel passing through the eye of a needle—a metaphor stark in its impossibility and hyperbolic illustration. This teaching challenges the disciples, and also us, to reflect on our attachments and the difficulty they present in genuinely following Jesus.

What would Jesus have you relinquish? For many of us, it's not money. Instead, it's the seduction of power and control. Our culture would have us believe we can control people, wealth, politics, nature, and the future. We seek to control time and destiny, story and meaning, history and education, money and privilege, politics and decisions, the earth and productivity, people and hope. We seek to exercise power and control through goal-setting, rhetoric, business, the military, monetary policy, religion, sexism, education, politics, legal instruments, and racial discrimination. In doing so, we abandon humility, trust, and surrender. So, what can we do? Repent of this passion for power. Surrender control. Return to dependence on God. Find fresh ways to honor the weak, foolish, dishonorable, and powerless. Determine to relinquish power. Embrace what it means to be "the filth of the world," whose approach to life seems foolish yet tells of another way.

The radical invitation extended by Jesus does not end in despair but in the promise that many who are first will be last and the last first. This inversion of worldly values is central to the gospel message. It invites us to find freedom not through accumulation but through relinquishment, not in exerting power but in embracing humility.

Big Idea: True spiritual freedom arises from letting go of our earthly attachments to embrace a life of radical discipleship.

Reflection: What does Jesus ask me to leave behind to follow him? How might my attachments be hindering my spiritual journey? How might I live more fully into the promise of the life that Jesus offers, a life marked not by the abundance of possessions but by the abundance of spirit and love?

Prayer: Lord, in our pursuit of you, teach us the grace of detachment from worldly goods so that we might find true riches in your love. Please help us to see the things we cling to that keep us from fully following you. Please give us the strength to release our grip on material wealth and comfort, opening our hands and hearts to receive the true abundance of a life lived in service to you and others. Amen.

Day 36

The Road to Jerusalem

Mark 10:32–34

As Jesus and his disciples journeyed toward Jerusalem, Jesus shared how he would suffer and later rise from the dead. A profound sense of destiny and solemnity marks this passage. Jesus leads the way, his steps resolute, and though the disciples follow, they are engulfed by a mix of awe and fear. Here, Jesus reveals to them the unfolding of events that await in Jerusalem—his betrayal, condemnation, death, and resurrection.

This moment vividly illustrates Jesus embracing his mission with unwavering commitment, fully aware of the suffering ahead. It's a powerful invitation to contemplate the depth of courage and love displayed by Jesus, who, knowing the cost, willingly walks towards it for the sake of humanity. This is the essence of self-giving love, which fully embraces suffering for the redemption of others.

For those of us following Christ, this passage calls us into a deeper understanding of discipleship. It challenges us to consider our paths: Are we ready to follow Jesus, not only to places of comfort and affirmation but also to areas of personal sacrifice and suffering? Do we grasp the weight of what it means to "take up our cross" and truly follow him? To serve is to be vulnerable and often to suffer. But God chose to be vulnerable in Jesus Christ so that we could see that in weakness, vulnerability, suffering, and humility, there is God's fullness of life and the surprising, transforming power of God.

This journey towards Jerusalem is not just a physical path but a spiritual journey towards the heart of the Christian faith—embracing suffering as a transformative power. In our lives, the road to Jerusalem can manifest in many forms: it may be the struggle to forgive, the challenge to serve others selflessly, or the call to stand up for justice and truth, even when it costs us dearly.

Suffering for Christ and his gospel can take many forms, but this story also reminds us of the promise and hope of resurrection. Though we suffer, we will be healed; though we are persecuted, we are loved; though we die, we will be raised to life.

As we reflect on this passage, let's ask for the grace to follow Christ with courage and love, trusting that through our journeys of suffering and sacrifice, we, too, may participate in the life-giving resurrection that follows. May we have the courage to walk our Jerusalem roads, led by the example of Christ who goes before us.

Big Idea: True discipleship entails following Jesus into suffering with a spirit of courage and transformative love. We live with the assurance that God will heal, love, and raise us.

Reflection: What does my "Jerusalem road" look like? Where is God calling me to embrace suffering or sacrifice for the sake of love and truth? How can I cultivate a heart willing to follow Jesus into difficult places, trusting in the transformative power of love and sacrifice?

Prayer: Lord Jesus, as you walked resolutely towards Jerusalem, grant us the courage to follow you on our paths of sacrifice. Teach us to embrace suffering not as a burden but as a sacred calling, a way to express our deepest love for you and others. Fill our hearts with the same resolve and compassion you showed, and we may not shy away from challenges but meet them with faith and trust.

MARK

May our journeys lead us closer to you and transform us, just as your path to Jerusalem transformed the world. In your name, we pray for strength and grace. Amen.

Day 37

Serving with Humility and Love

Mark 10:35-45

It's easy for us to misunderstand Jesus and the nature of his kingdom. We're tempted to form a vision of Christ and his kingdom in our image, reflecting our understanding of honor, status, and power. In this passage, James and John approach Jesus with a request that reveals their misunderstanding of the true nature of his kingdom. They ask for positions of glory alongside him, not grasping the full implications of their journey with Christ. Jesus responds with a question about their ability to share in his suffering, highlighting the profound disconnect between their desires for status and the path of servanthood he embodies. We often seek status instead of suffering, honor instead of humility, and power instead of servanthood.

Jesus then gathers all his disciples to teach a fundamental lesson about the nature of authentic leadership and greatness, which contrasts sharply with worldly notions. "Whoever wants to become great among you shall be your servant. Whoever of you wants to become first among you, shall be bondservant of all" (vv. 34-34). Here, Jesus redefines greatness as a measure of service, not power, of giving oneself away, not accumulating honor or

89

accolades. Jesus inverts status and honor in his description of the kingdom of God, showing that God opposes the proud but gives grace to the humble, elevating those whom religions and societies often despise and overlook. The qualities that God prizes and that characterize God's kingdom are frequently different than those prized by religious, political, and social powers and structures.

Jesus's teaching invites us to reflect deeply on our aspirations and motivations. In a world that often equates greatness with power, control, and visibility, Jesus presents an alternative vision where true greatness is found in humility, service, and sacrificial love. This kingdom perspective challenges us to examine how we perceive success and influence in our lives and communities.

The example of Jesus, who came "not to be served, but to serve, and to give his life as a ransom for many" (v. 45), is a radical call to all who follow him. It invites us into a life where power is understood as the capacity to uplift others, leadership is about empowering rather than dominating, and our highest calling is to serve those around us, particularly the least, the last, and the lost. If we have eyes to see, we will notice God's presence among the humble and lowly, as the Spirit of Christ honors those who relinquish earthly power, control, and status, and instead choose to pursue the righteousness, humility, and servanthood of Christ. Jesus invites us to shift from seeking to be first to putting ourselves last, from desiring accolades to living out the quiet, unnoticed acts of kindness and service that resonate with the heart of the gospel.

Big Idea: True greatness in the kingdom of God is measured by our willingness to serve others with humility and love.

Reflection: In what areas of my life can I move from seeking personal accolades to embracing the role of a servant? How does Jesus's model of servant leadership challenge my current understanding and practice of power and influence?

Prayer: Loving God, who came not to be served but to serve, instill in us the spirit of true humility and selfless service. Forgive us for the times we've grasped after status, power, control, and honor. Please help us to see ministry, leadership, and discipleship as an opportunity to serve rather than to be exalted. Teach us to value the well-being of others above our desires for recognition, embracing the least and the lost as you did. May our lives reflect your sacrificial love, and may we find joy in the quiet acts of service that go unnoticed by the world but are cherished in your sight. Guide us to be great in your kingdom by being servants to all. Amen.

Day 38

Seeing with Faith

Mark 10:46-52

In a dramatic scene, Jesus encounters Bartimaeus, a blind beggar sitting by the roadside. Bartimaeus is a man who lives at the fringes of his society, suffering all the exclusions and prejudices that come with the double challenges of poverty and physical ailment. When Bartimaeus hears that it is Jesus of Nazareth, he shouts, "Jesus, you Son of David, have mercy on me!" (v. 47). Bartimaeus instinctively knows that Jesus is the promised Messiah, the Son of David who comes to heal and save, the one sent from God clothed with compassion, mercy, and power. He calls out even more fervently despite many rebuking him and telling him to be silent. Moved by his cry, Jesus stops and says, "Call him" (v. 49). When Bartimaeus is called, he throws off his cloak, springs up, and comes to Jesus. Jesus asks him, "What do you want me to do for you?" The blind man says, "Rabboni, that I may see again" (v. 51). Jesus responds, "Go your way. Your faith has made you well" (v. 52). Immediately, he regains his sight and follows Jesus on the way. This is a striking story filled with human need and faith, as well as divine mercy and supremacy.

This story is rich with spiritual depth, inviting us to reflect on our spiritual blindness and cries for mercy. Bartimaeus, in his physical blindness, recognizes Jesus more profoundly than many with sight, and his faith and persistence in seeking Jesus's mercy teach us about the nature of true discipleship. Do we see Jesus for who he is? Do we believe he loves us and has the power to heal and liberate us? Will we make ourselves vulnerable and even foolish for the sake of naming who Jesus is and expressing our faith in him?

The cloak Bartimaeus throws off can be seen as a symbol of all we cling to that keeps us in darkness—the fears, insecurities, past hurts, or sins we wrap around ourselves for comfort or protection. His throwing it aside to come to Jesus is a powerful metaphor for the renunciation required to follow Jesus fully. Do we throw these things aside, trusting that God is sufficient and good? Or do we cling to them, staying in the spiritual darkness or sickness that keeps us bound?

Jesus's question to Bartimaeus, "What do you want me to do for you?" is also posed to each of us. It invites us to discern our deepest longing and bring it to Jesus in faith. Bartimaeus's request to see again is not just for physical sight but for a new way of seeing the world, transformed by the touch of Christ.

As we journey with Jesus, may we have the courage to throw off whatever hinders us, to cry out for mercy, and to follow him with renewed vision and faith, seeing the world and our place in it with the eyes of the heart enlightened.

Big Idea: True sight requires throwing off our burdens and seeking Jesus with a heart full of faith.

Reflection: What "cloaks" do I need to throw off to see the way of Jesus more clearly? How does my faith influence my ability to see and respond to the needs around me?

Prayer: Lord Jesus, the one who responded to Bartimaeus's cry for mercy, hear our prayers as we seek to follow you more closely. Please help us to cast aside the burdens that close our eyes to your presence and the needs of others. Grant us the courage to call out to you in our need and the faith to trust in your healing touch.

May we see the world anew with eyes of faith, compassion, and understanding, following you on the path of discipleship with hearts unencumbered and spirits renewed. In your loving name, we pray. Amen.

Day 39

Welcoming Christ's Reign

Mark 11:1-11

The triumphant entry of Jesus into Jerusalem is rich with spiritual and symbolic meaning. As Jesus rides into the city on a colt, fulfilling the prophecy of Zechariah, the crowd spreads their cloaks on the road, waves branches cut from the fields, and cries out "Hosanna." This act of spreading cloaks might seem a simple gesture, but it signifies something profound: a laying down of oneself, an offering of one's life and possessions in honor of someone greater.

This scene invites us to reflect on our responses to Jesus's presence in our lives. How do we welcome Jesus? Do we lay down our cloaks—our plans, comforts, and securities—to honor him? Do we recognize his arrival in the quiet moments, in the faces of those we encounter, in the challenges and joys we face each day? Are we eagerly expecting his presence and reign? Are we willing to lay aside our ambitions and strivings so that Christ may be glorified, and his kingdom and salvation may come?

The people's shouts of "Hosanna!"—a plea for salvation—express their deep longing for deliverance. Every part of their cry was rooted in the Hebrew tradition and laden with messianic expectations. These acclamations reflect the deep yearning among Jews of the period for political, social, and spiritual redemption.

In the context of Jesus's entry into Jerusalem, they signify the widespread hope that Jesus was the promised Davidic Messiah who would fulfill these deeply held expectations. However, the nature of Jesus's mission and kingdom—focused on spiritual salvation and transformation rather than political liberation—was a point of eventual contention and misunderstanding among many of his contemporaries. The expectations of a political savior were soon to be turned upside down. Jesus came not to overthrow earthly powers with force but to conquer hearts through love and establish a kingdom not of domination but of peace. Jesus wasn't only the Messiah for the Jewish people but the One from God who had come to forgive, redeem, and welcome all the peoples of the earth into God's salvation and kingdom.

As we enter the spirit of this passage, let us consider our expectations of Jesus. Are we open to the unexpected ways in which he works? Do we allow him to enter the Jerusalem of our hearts and set up his reign of peace and love? Are we prepared to follow Jesus not just in moments of triumphant procession but also to the cross? In welcoming Jesus, let's spread before him not just our cloaks but our very selves, offering our lives as pathways for his love to enter the world. In this way, we genuinely celebrate Jesus's coming and participate in the profound mystery of his saving work.

Big Idea: Welcoming Jesus into our lives calls for profoundly surrendering our desires and expectations, inviting his transformative love to reign in our hearts.

Reflection: What expectations and images of Jesus do I need to let go of? How can I remain open to the unexpected ways Jesus manifests his kingdom among the people in my society and my daily experiences?

Prayer: Lord Jesus, as you entered Jerusalem to cries of "Hosanna," enter our hearts with your quiet and loving yet messianic and transforming presence. Please help us lay down our lives before you, surrendering our desires, plans, and expectations at your feet. Teach us to welcome you not just with words but through our actions and choices, making our lives a testimony to your love and peace. May we not seek you only in triumph but follow you even to the cross, trusting in your way of humble service and sacrificial love. Amen.

Day 40

Beyond Appearances,
Into Prayer

Mark 11:12–26

This passage presents two challenging scenes that reveal Jesus's deep desire for spiritual authenticity. First, we find Jesus cursing a fig tree for its lack of fruit despite it being in full leaf. Later, he enters the temple and drives out those who have turned this sacred space into a marketplace, declaring that it should be "a house of prayer for all the nations" (v. 17). These two events seem harsh and disconnected at first glance, but they expose something profound: God desires more than mere appearances. God investigates the heart and sees things as they are, wanting justice, mercy, humility, integrity, and faithfulness.

With its leaves but no fruit, the fig tree becomes a symbol of the spiritual pretense that looks healthy on the outside but is barren within. In an age where people curate their image, Jesus reminds us that what looks good on the outside can often be barren, deceptive, and unfruitful on the inside. Similarly, the bustling activity in the temple could easily deceive onlookers into thinking it was spiritually alive. Yet, Jesus discerns a hollowness and corruption at its core—where personal gain, not prayer, has taken root. Jesus is angered in both instances, using these encounters to teach his disciples less about spiritual authenticity and virtue and possibly offering a visual commentary on the barrenness and corruption of the Jewish ethnic, social, and religious imagination, practices, and institutions. Jesus challenges his disciples to be different.

These scenes challenge us to examine our own lives. Are we bearing the fruit of God's love, or are we content with looking good on the outside while ignoring the more profound work of spiritual transformation within? The world encourages us to curate and present our image and brand and to lead superficial, egotistical, and busy lives that don't leave room for spiritual depth. Do we allow prayer to anchor our lives or fill our hearts with distractions that keep us from true communion with God?

Jesus's command to "have faith in God" and to pray boldly invites us into a renewed relationship with the Divine. By setting aside the things that clutter our hearts, encourage our image curation, and prevent our authentic growth, we can allow God's presence to flourish within us. But this takes solitude, silence, reflection, and accountability within a genuine community. Just as Jesus cleared the temple, he desires to cleanse our lives of anything that hinders us from fruitful discipleship. Notice that Jesus links bold faith and genuine prayer with forgiveness. Again, Jesus gets to the heart of the matter, reminding us that God sees deeply into our hearts and wants integrity and righteousness. May we seek not just to appear spiritually alive but to cultivate lives that genuinely reflect God's love. In doing so, we become like the house of prayer that Jesus envisions—a place where faith, forgiveness, and prayer grow freely.

Big Idea: Jesus wants us to cleanse our hearts of distractions and pretense, making room for God's transformative love.

Reflection: What things deep in my heart keep me from authentic spiritual growth and bearing fruit in my relationship with God? How can I incorporate a deeper practice of prayer into my daily life to nurture my faith? Where does God want me to exercise bold faith and genuine forgiveness?

Prayer: Gracious God, you call us to fruitful lives, pure hearts, forgiving relationships, bold faith, and spiritual authenticity. Please cleanse my heart as you cleansed the temple, removing all that prevents me from bearing the fruits of love, joy, and faithfulness. Lead me beyond spiritual pretense and image curation into genuine communion with you. Please help me recognize the clutter, superficiality, unforgiveness, and doubt that distract me from your presence and give me the courage to remove it. May your love transform my inner being so I may become a vessel of your grace, forgiveness, and gospel. Guide me to create a house of prayer within, where your Spirit flourishes. Amen.

Day 41

Surrender to God's Authority

Mark 11:27-33

Fear and pride can often intermingle. Combined, they can close our hearts to God's ways, cause us to be skeptical and dogmatic, lead us into deceptive and uncompassionate actions, and prevent us from being honest and straightforward. When fear and pride characterize our religiosity, they damage our ability to trust and recognize God's activity, love, and authority.

In this passage, we see Jesus questioned by the chief priests, teachers of the law, and elders about the authority behind his actions. Their focus is not on truth or understanding but on trapping him. The religious leaders confront Jesus with a question designed to ensnare: "By what authority do you do these things?" (v. 28). Yet, using wisdom and clever rhetoric, Jesus responds with his question about John the Baptist's baptism. In doing so, Jesus exposes their fear of losing control and reveals their unwillingness to answer truthfully.

This story invites us to examine our hearts. Are we open to recognizing God's authority in the world and at work in our lives? Or do we seek to control and defend our preconceived notions? The chief priests and elders, deceived by their desire for self-preservation, were unable to perceive the authority of God's love embodied in Jesus Christ.

Often, we approach our faith with similar fears. And when our fears combine with pride and a desire for control, our words and actions fail to glorify God or serve humanity and creation. We long for certainty yet struggle to surrender control. We seek affirmation for our assumptions and carefully curated image rather than opening ourselves to the deeper mystery of God's power, grace, and presence. But Jesus invites us to a posture of humility and trust—a willingness to follow him even when it challenges our deeply held beliefs.

True faith is not about having all the answers but about living in a relationship of loving surrender. Genuine openness to God involves receiving the way God works unexpectedly and among the least likely people, without asking fearfully and pridefully, "By whose authority are these things done?" When we acknowledge God's authority in our lives, we release our tight grip on control and embrace a path of openness. Here, we find the freedom to trust and love deeply. We learn to approach God's presence not with a spirit of control but with an open heart, willing to receive, trust, and surrender to Christ's authority. By seeking first the kingdom of God and laying down our need to grasp tightly, we encounter a love that removes all fear, a grace that liberates, and a divine presence that humbles and transforms.

Big Idea: Acknowledging God's authority requires surrendering our pride, fears, and need for control. Jesus invites us to embrace a trust in God's authority and love that transforms us.

Reflection: What deeply held beliefs, fear, or pride might prevent me from fully surrendering to God's authority? How can I foster a deeper spirit of trust and openness in my relationship with God?

Prayer: Loving Father, release my spirit from the grasp of control, fear, and pride. Please prevent me from approaching you with preconceived notions and self preserving fears, or treating others

SURRENDER TO GOD'S AUTHORITY

with contempt, fear, and dominance. Guard my heart from the worst forms of religious arrogance. Instead, please help me yield my heart entirely to your authority. Help me embrace the uncertainty of faith with humility and openness, trusting that your grace and wisdom will guide my every step. Soften my heart for your transforming love that liberates, humbles, and renews. Teach me daily to lean into your guidance, allowing your kingdom to flourish. Amen.

Day 42

Honoring the Beloved Son

Mark 12:1-12

In Mark 12, Jesus tells the parable of the wicked tenants, depicting a vineyard owner who leases his vineyard to tenants. When the owner sends servants to collect his due, the tenants abuse and kill them. It's a violent, captivating, provocative story. Finally, he sends his beloved son, thinking they will respect him, but they kill him too, believing they can seize the inheritance. Jesus concludes by speaking of the stone the builders rejected becoming the cornerstone, a metaphor revealing God's redemptive plan and the treatment and nature of the Son of God.

The story is a commentary on the Jew's treatment of Jesus, God's redemptive plan for humanity, and the vindication of Christ through God's judgment. It's a provocation and prophecy, and it infuriates the religious leaders. But if we zoom out further, we see how this story illustrates the way humanity often struggles with the gift of the gospel and divine love. The vineyard represents God's generous provision, and the tenants' behavior mirrors our tendency to prioritize our desires, disregarding the call to stewardship and obedience. By rejecting the owner's son, the tenants embody our rejection of the divine gospel and transformative invitation Jesus offers us.

We often live as if God's vineyard is our own, forgetting the One to whom we truly belong. We build, plant, sow, and harvest and see ourselves as masters of our fields, fortunes, and destinies. We develop monuments to our egos and achievements. We turn away from the Lord of the vineyards and harvest, even while giving lip service to Christ. We see ourselves as strong, independent, and self-determined instead of humble, dependent, and guided by the will and purposes of the vigneron (the winemaker who nurtures the vineyard and makes the new wine). The rejection of the cornerstone is a vivid reminder that we can reject the very thing that brings life in seeking to control our lives. Jesus is the cornerstone. But in this parable, grace shines through. Despite the tenants' rebellion, God's purposes remain unshaken. The rejected cornerstone becomes the foundation of new life.

This passage challenges us to let go of our tight grip on our ambitions and egos and instead embrace a life of stewardship, dependence, gratitude, and humility. In Christ, the rejected cornerstone, we find a foundation of love that calls us to radical transformation and surrender. May we learn to receive the vineyard of God's love with open hands, stewarding it faithfully and gratefully. Let's recognize and celebrate the beloved Son, the cornerstone of our faith, embracing his call to build a kingdom of justice and compassion where God's love and grace can flourish.

Big Idea: Recognizing Christ as the cornerstone requires letting go of ego, plans, and control and humbly receiving the divine gift of God's gospel and vineyard.

Reflection: In what areas of my life am I struggling to surrender control to God, mistakenly believing that the vineyard is mine to own? How can I live as a faithful steward, building God's kingdom of justice, love, and compassion?

Prayer: Gracious Winemaker, we acknowledge your vineyard is not ours to control but yours to provide. You are the harvest's Lord, the vineyard's owner, the gospel's giver, our soul's lover, humanity's savior, and creation's designer. Forgive us when we reject the cornerstone in pursuing selfish ambitions and egotistical monuments. Guide us to live as grateful stewards, honoring your beloved Son and the kingdom he came to establish. May our hearts be rooted in humility, gratitude, and grace, and may we be willing to receive your love as the ultimate foundation. Please help us build with compassion and care, trusting your redemptive purposes even when we struggle to let go. We need your help to be humble, trusting, thankful servants of your will. We desire to see your kingdom flourish in our lives and our world. Amen.

Day 43

Living beyond Worldly Limitations

Mark 12:13-27

The Pharisees, Herodians, and Sadducees pose challenging questions to Jesus, trying to trap him. The first question is about taxes, and Jesus answers that we should give to secular authorities what belongs to them and to God what belongs to God. It's a clever answer because we often submit to secular and political authorities as an act of integrity and witness while recognizing that all things belong to the Creator and Lord of humanity and the whole cosmos. Later, the Sadducees pose a hypothetical scenario to ridicule the concept of resurrection, asking whose wife a woman who had married seven brothers would be after the resurrection. Jesus counters their faulty logic, affirming the resurrection by reminding them of God's words: "I am the God of Abraham, the God of Isaac, and the God of Jacob" (v. 26). God will transform relationships and social structures in the resurrection, God's promises transcend death, and God's covenants are eternal. We should see life through the lens of eternity and the nature of God, with God's promises and covenants enduring beyond this world.

Secular and religious politics consumed the imagination of the religious leaders. Their hearts were hardened to God, the Spirit, divine power, and the Scriptures. Jesus reveals a heavenly wisdom that transcends the trickery and limited understanding of his challengers and political machinations. Earthly politics consumed the Pharisees, and a narrow, skeptical worldview constrained the Sadducees. Yet, Jesus teaches us to hold these things lightly, refocusing on what truly matters: God's eternal plans and promises and our relationship with God.

Jesus's response reminds us that while we have duties to society and obligations to powers and rulers, our ultimate allegiance is to God. Jesus invites us to look beyond the daily disputes that seek to trap us and to root our lives in the eternal reality of God's promises and love. Furthermore, the affirmation of resurrection calls us to live with an unshakeable hope that death does not have the final word.

Jesus's question in verse 24 is fascinating: "Isn't this because you are mistaken, not knowing the Scriptures, nor the power of God?" We're often tempted to focus on one or the other: the power of the Spirit or the truth of God's Scriptures. But we need both to lead lives of truth, power, and faithfulness to Jesus Christ.

Big Idea: Our allegiance to God's eternal kingdom requires us to see beyond worldly structures and trust the life-giving power of God's promises, nature, and resurrection.

Reflection: What areas of my life are rooted in worldly expectations or outlooks that prevent me from fully embracing God's transformative promises? Am I living in the power of God and the truth of the Scriptures? How can I shift my perspective to cultivate an unshakeable hope in the resurrection, grounding myself in God's eternal nature, covenant, and love?

Prayer: Lord Jesus Christ, your wisdom transcends earthly understanding and invites us into a kingdom of boundless hope and eternal promises. Let us find peace in your promise of resurrection, where the joy of everlasting life undoes sorrow. Help us live in God's power and the truth and liberation of the Scriptures. As we consider the politics and tensions of this world, give us the grace to release our fears and place our trust in your eternal love. May we recognize the power of your promises and dwell firmly in the assurance that you are the God of the living and all of eternity. Lead us in becoming true citizens of your kingdom, where your love, will, and power rule supreme. Please fill our hearts with faith, hope, and love. Amen.

Day 44

Heartfelt Love and Humble Giving

Mark 12:28–44

The teachings of Jesus redefine how we see the world and spirituality, often shattering our understandings and expectations. In this passage, Jesus teaches about the love of God and neighbors (the greatest commandments), the supremacy of the Messiah even over revered figures of the Jewish faith, the destructiveness of religious hypocrisy and self-promotion, and God's esteem for those who give faithfully out of the little or abundance they have.

When religious leaders ask Jesus about the greatest commandment in the Jewish law, he replies with the simple yet transformative: "Love the Lord your God with all your heart, with all your soul, with all your mind, and with all your strength" (vv. 29–30). This call to love God wholly means surrendering and giving our lives entirely to an intimate, transformative relationship with God. Jesus invites us to a divine-human relationship of deep intimacy, profound renewal, and unwavering devotion. It means allowing every part of our being to be touched and transformed by God's truth, righteousness, grace, and love.

The second commandment, "Love your neighbor as yourself," (v. 31) flows naturally from the first. How can we say we love

God but do not love our neighbors? Our love for God cannot be separated from our love for others. It is in the small acts of kindness, the moments of compassion, the decisions to be hospitable and generous, and the willingness to serve that we truly reflect the love of God. This love is not about grand gestures but about a consistent, humble presence in the lives of those around us.

Jesus reshapes his hearers' understandings of Scripture, showing how the Messiah's authority exceeds even that of revered figures in the Jewish faith and tradition. While the Messiah is a descendant of David, his is greater than David's. Jesus is the Messiah who fulfills the Scriptures not only through lineage or earthly power but through his divine nature and authority ordained by God.

Jesus then observes a widow in the temple, who gives two small coins—everything she must live on. This woman doesn't have much money but gives all she has. Her offering, though seemingly insignificant, is profound in its totality. God sees and honors her. Unlike the rich, who give out of their abundance and for show, she gives out of her poverty, with humility and faithfulness. Giving all she has embodies the essence of Jesus's commandments: loving God and others with everything we are and have. Again, Jesus uses everyday people and situations to reshape our understanding of God, Scripture, and Christ's kingdom.

In these passages, we are challenged to reflect on the depth of our love and the sincerity of our offerings. Are we loving God with our whole being? Are we loving our neighbors as ourselves? And in our giving, whether of time, resources, or compassion, are we offering from a place of abundance or true sacrifice? May Jesus's teachings and the story of the widow's offering inspire us to lead lives marked by profound love and generous self-giving. We can trust God's love and faithfulness, knowing that as we give all, we find our true treasure in the heart of God.

Big Idea: Jesus the Messiah transcends our earthly expectations, showing us that genuine love and humble generosity reveal the heart of true discipleship.

Reflection: How can I cultivate a love for God that encompasses all my heart, soul, mind, and strength? How might this be expressed in my love for neighbors, strangers, and enemies? How can I practice humble generosity, giving not from abundance but from the depths of my heart?

Prayer: Jesus the Messiah, please teach us the depth of true love, the supremacy of your lordship, and the beauty of humble giving. Please help us love you with all our heart, soul, mind, and strength, and love our neighbors, strangers, and even enemies as ourselves. In our giving, may we reflect the widow's offering, giving from the depths of our hearts and trusting in your presence, power, provision, protection, and providence. Transform our lives through the power of your love, and let our actions reveal the heart of true discipleship. Amen.

Day 45

Hope amid Turmoil

Mark 13

Mark 13 is an unusual and unsettling chapter. Jesus speaks with his disciples about the end times and the coming of the kingdom of God. Amidst the grandeur and apparent permanence of the temple, Jesus points to more profound, lasting truths, emphasizing the transience of earthly structures and the importance of spiritual vigilance. Jesus covers many issues that require spiritual alertness, boldness, and trust. These include signs of the end times, the destruction of religious monuments, wars and human catastrophes, persecution, relational discord, false messiahs and prophets, and the coming of the Son of Man in great glory and power. Jesus challenges us to read the signs of the times, be spiritually vigilant and faithful, and "Watch!"

Jesus describes the profound disruptions that will precede the end—wars, earthquakes, famines, false messiahs, family breakdown, betrayal, and persecutions. Yet, Christ focuses not on cultivating fear but on encouraging watchfulness and faith. Be vigilant. Fear not. Stay faithful. Proclaim the gospel. Guard against deception. Endure suffering with hope. Be on guard and alert. Ensure your heart and spirit remain focused on God amid chaos and uncertainty. Preach the gospel to all nations. Expect sacrilegious acts that offend God and lead to destruction ("the abomination of desolation," Matt 24:15), but know that God's power, holiness, justice, righteousness, will, and glory will prevail.

This passage invites us to reflect on how we anticipate God's kingdom. It challenges us to consider what it means to stay spiritually alert daily. Are we attentive to the ways God is speaking to us now, or are we distracted by the anxieties and pressures of our world? How do we maintain our faith when facing metaphorical and literal earthquakes and storms? Are we keeping watch, as instructed by the owner of this metaphorical house, knowing that our Lord will return?

Jesus's teaching in Mark 13 is not just a prophetic warning about the future but a call to live fully in the present, with our hearts anchored in the promise of God's enduring faithfulness. It reminds us that our ultimate hope is not in our surroundings' stability but God's unshakable kingdom. Our role isn't to preserve earthly or religious structures but to proclaim the gospel of Jesus Christ and stay spiritually vigilant and faithful. No matter what we face in life, we can find comfort in the assurance that though the earth may shake and the heavens may fall, the word of God stands forever. Christ's words are trustworthy and eternal. We can live each day with purpose and readiness, embodying the love and peace of the kingdom we await. The Spirit of Christ urges us to watch and pray, not out of fear, but with a spirit of profound hope and joy, as we anticipate the complete revelation of God's glory.

Big Idea: In times of conflict, chaos, and crisis, our spiritual vigilance and unwavering hope in God's eternal promises sustain us.

Reflection: How can I cultivate a spirit of watchfulness that keeps me attuned to God's presence and guidance? What practices help me maintain hope and faith during uncertainty and fear?

Prayer: Loving God, please help us watch and stay alert, even when we see terrifying and unsettling events and signs of the times. In the swirling chaos of our world, please anchor us firmly in your eternal promises. Teach us to watch and pray with hearts full of hope, not dismay. In moments of fear and uncertainty, remind us of your steadfast presence and kingdom that transcends all earthly strife. Please help us trust in your ultimate plan: in every ending, there is a new beginning and an opportunity for renewal in every trial. May we hold fast to the hope of your coming kingdom, living each day as a testament to your love and grace. Amen.

Day 46

Devotion and Betrayal

Mark 14:1–31

Mark 14 offers poignant and intimate moments leading up to Jesus's arrest and crucifixion. This passage is rich with themes of love, betrayal, and ultimate sacrifice.

As the chapter begins, we see the chief priests and teachers of the religious law form a plot to arrest Jesus by stealth and kill him. In contrast to this evil scheme, Mark presents us with a story about a beautiful act of devotion. A woman approaches Jesus with an alabaster jar of very costly perfume and pours it on Jesus's head. Her act of anointing Jesus is met with indignation by some present, who see it as wasteful—or at least that's the explanation they give each other for their annoyance with the woman. Yet, Jesus defends her, saying, "She has done a beautiful thing to me . . . She poured perfume on my body beforehand to prepare for my burial. Truly I tell you, wherever the gospel is preached throughout the world, what she has done will also be told, in memory of her" (vv. 6–9, NIV). The significance of her devoted, pre-crucifixion act glorifies Jesus Christ, responds to the leading of the Holy Spirit, aligns with the will of the Father, is praised by the heavenly hosts, and will be remembered throughout history.

This woman's act of love and sacrifice stands in sharp relief against the looming betrayal of Judas, who soon after agrees to betray Jesus for thirty pieces of silver. The juxtaposition of these two acts—a pure, selfless devotion and a cold, calculated betrayal—highlights our choices in our spiritual journeys. Are we willing to pour out our lives in devotion, or do we find ourselves tempted by the allure of self-preservation and gain? The men in this story—religious leaders and disciples—struggle to glorify Christ. But the woman with the alabaster jar and oil shows holy, pure, loving devotion to Jesus, bringing honor and glory to Christ before his crucifixion.

As we move to the Last Supper, Jesus shares a meal with his disciples, breaking bread and offering wine as symbols of his body and blood poured out for many. Here, Jesus institutes the Eucharist, a profound mystery of love, sacrifice, and divine-human communion in which we are invited to participate, remembering Christ's ultimate act of love.

During this meal, Jesus also predicts Peter's denial. Despite Peter's pride and vehement protests, Jesus calmly foretells that Peter will deny him three times before the rooster crows twice. This prediction, filled with sorrow and compassion, speaks to our human frailty. Jesus understands our frailty and weaknesses. Even in our most decisive moments of resolve, we can falter, doubt, and deny Jesus. Yet, Jesus's foreknowledge and continued love for Peter remind us of his bottomless compassion, understanding, and forgiveness.

In the stories in this chapter, the Spirit invites us to reflect on our acts of betrayal, frailty, remembrance, faithfulness, and devotion. How do we respond to Jesus's love? Are our hearts open and devoted? Do we follow the leading of the Spirit? Will we accept Jesus's compassion when we falter and are weak? Are we willing to offer our lives in humble service and devotion, like the woman with the alabaster jar? Can we acknowledge our weaknesses and seek forgiveness, as Peter eventually does? Let's pray for the grace to lead lives of genuine devotion, recognizing the immense love that Jesus pours out for us. May we find strength in Jesus's example, courage in his sacrifice, and hope in his resurrection.

Big Idea: Our response to Jesus's love calls us to acts of devotion and recognition of our frailty.

Reflection: How can I offer my life more fully in devotion to Jesus, like the woman with the alabaster jar? Following Peter's example, how do I confront and seek forgiveness for my moments of weakness and betrayal?

Prayer: Lord Jesus, thank you for showing us how to face betrayal with forgiveness, compassion, and love. Please help us to respond with devotion and humility. Teach us to pour out our lives as an offering. We want to honor you in all we do. Please remind us of your compassionate understanding and boundless grace in our moments of weakness. You always reach out to us, love us, forgive us, and offer us a fresh start. Grant us the courage to seek forgiveness and the strength to follow you more closely. May our lives reflect the deep love you have shown us as we strive to live out your call with faithfulness and humility. Amen.

Day 47

Gethsemane's Lesson
of Surrender

Mark 14:32–72

In Mark 14:32–72, we journey with Jesus through some of his most agonizing moments, offering profound insights into the depths of his humanity and the boundless reach of his love. This passage invites us to sit with Jesus in Gethsemane, witness his betrayal and arrest, and observe the denial by Peter, his closest disciple.

At Gethsemane, Jesus takes Peter, James, and John aside and becomes profoundly distressed and troubled. "My soul is exceedingly sorrowful, even to death," he confides (v. 34). In this moment, we can see our own struggles mirrored in Jesus's vulnerability. His plea in verse 26, "Abba, Father, all things are possible to you. Please remove this cup from me. However, not what I desire, but what you desire," captures the profound struggle between his human desire to avoid suffering and his divine mission to embrace the cross for our redemption. We see Jesus's intimacy with his Father, his human struggle before his crucifixion, and, like his disciples, his wrestle between his flesh and spirit. Yet, Jesus is resolved to do the will of his Abba Father.

Despite his anguish, Jesus's acceptance of God's will invites us to reflect on our own struggles with surrender. How often do we cling to our desires, resisting God's path before us? In Jesus's prayer, we find a model of trust and obedience, a call to relinquish our will for God's greater plan.

As Jesus is arrested, betrayed by Judas with a kiss, and led away, we see the culmination of his path of suffering begin. The disciples scatter, and Peter, following at a distance, soon faces his own trial of loyalty. Peter's three denials, punctuated by the crowing rooster, remind us of our own frailties. Despite his bold promises, Peter falls into fear and self-preservation. Yet, even in this moment of failure, we are not left in despair. Jesus had foretold Peter's denial with a heart full of understanding and love, hinting at the forgiveness and restoration to come.

Throughout these passages, we are confronted with the stark contrasts of human weakness and divine strength, of flesh and spirit, of evil and holiness, and of betrayal and unwavering love. Jesus, in his vulnerability, shows us the depth of his solidarity with our human condition while also revealing the power of divine love to transform and redeem. Let's pray for the grace to trust in God's plan, to seek forgiveness when we falter, and to follow Jesus's example of love and obedience, even in the face of suffering. This call to trust and seek forgiveness is not a onetime action but a continuous journey that inspires faith and determination.

Big Idea: In Jesus's surrender and suffering, we find a model of trust, love, and redemption for our weaknesses.

Reflection: How can I practice surrendering my will to embrace God's plan, even when it leads to discomfort or suffering? How do I seek forgiveness and restoration in my moments of failure, inspired by Peter's journey?

Prayer: Lord, in the garden of Gethsemane, you showed us the depths of your sorrow and the heights of your obedience. Teach us to trust in your will, even when it leads us through valleys of suffering and doubt. Please help us to surrender our desires and fears, embracing the path you have set before us. In our moments of weakness, may we remember Peter's denial and your forgiveness, finding hope in your boundless love. Strengthen us to follow you with unwavering faith, knowing your love redeems and restores. Amen.

Day 48

Silent Strength in Suffering

Mark 15:1-20

Mark describes Jesus's trial before Pilate, his condemnation, and the cruel mockery he endures. This story is filled with suffering and injustice, inviting us to contemplate the profound mystery of Jesus's silent endurance, self-sacrifice, and boundless love.

Jesus stands before Pilate, accused by the chief priests, yet he's silent, offering no defense. Pilate, perplexed by his silence, succumbs to the crowd's demands, releasing Barabbas and condemning Jesus to crucifixion. At this moment, we see Jesus as the suffering servant, fulfilling the prophecy of Isaiah: "He was oppressed, yet when he was afflicted he didn't open his mouth. As a lamb that is led to the slaughter, and as a sheep that before its shearers is silent, so he didn't open his mouth" (Isa 53:7).

The soldiers take Jesus into the palace, where they mock him, placing a crown of thorns on his head and dressing him in a purple robe. Their actions, meant to humiliate, ironically affirm Jesus's true kingship. Amid their taunts, Jesus remains silent, embodying a love transcending human cruelty. How often do we offend Christ with sarcasm, cynicism, and mocking attitudes? It's easy to pass judgment on the soldiers, but we're frequently guilty of our forms of cynicism and mockery, insulting Christ and the Spirit and disappointing God. Still, Jesus shows us the generosity of God, who loves despite our cynicism, forgives despite our failings, and heals despite the wounds we inflict on Jesus. I am Pilate. I sound like the soldiers. I look and act like the religious leaders and the crowds. Yet, Jesus loves, heals, forgives, and embraces me.

This passage invites us to reflect on our responses to suffering and injustice. Jesus's silence is not a sign of weakness, but a profound strength rooted in his trust in God's will. But when we read the Gospels, we see that Jesus wasn't always silent. We must consider carefully how we respond to evil, injustice, and suffering and how we might embrace our trials with a similar spirit of courage, determination, surrender, and love. The Spirit will lead us—to speak or be silent and to act or patiently wait.

We often encounter situations where we are tempted to defend ourselves, fight back against injustices we face, and refuse and challenge the wrongful sufferings of ourselves and others. There are certainly times when that's timely, necessary, and appropriate. But Jesus shows us a different way—silence and patience. The Spirit of Christ may call us to act or wait, to speak up or be silent. Either way, we must trust in God's ultimate justice and love. As we meditate on Christ's passion, we ask God for the grace to endure our trials with a heart full of love and trust, knowing that we are united with God in our suffering.

Big Idea: Jesus's silent endurance in suffering reveals the profound strength of trusting God's will.

Reflection: How can I cultivate a spirit of trust and surrender in the face of my trials and injustices? How do I discern when it's the time to act, wait, speak, or be silent? What does Jesus's silence teach me about responding to suffering with love and faith?

Prayer: Lord Jesus Christ, in the face of suffering and injustice, you remained silent, trusting God's will. Please teach us to endure our trials with the same strength and love. Please help us to see beyond our pain to the greater purpose you have for us. May we find comfort in your presence and courage to follow your example, embracing our cross with faith and love. Amen.

Day 49

Love's Ultimate Sacrifice

Mark 15:21-47

Crucifixion is a humiliating and painful death. There are at least three intertwined dimensions of crucifixion: physical suffering, public humiliation, and social and spiritual degradation. Jesus's physical suffering was excruciating. The soldiers whipped him and nailed him to a cross, driving the nails through his wrists and feet, subjecting him to immense physical agony, and killing him through torture, dehydration, shock, and eventual asphyxiation. The public humiliation was central to crucifixion. Jesus was stripped naked, spat on, and ridiculed by soldiers and passersby. The intention is to degrade the person crucified, and the soldiers top this off with a crown of thorns and a purple robe and sarcastically call him the "King of the Jews." The social and spiritual degradation is even deeper than the physical suffering and public humiliation. The Jews saw crucifixion as a curse (Deut 21:23). The Jews understood those crucified to be abandoned by God, spiritually cursed and degraded, and disgraced beyond all measure.

I describe these aspects of Jesus's crucifixion in detail because we often read the story of the crucifixion without perceiving its horror, pain, humiliation, and disgrace. In Mark 15:1-20, we stand with Jesus as he faces the profound injustice of his trial and the cruel mockery of the soldiers. Pilate, though finding no fault in Jesus, succumbs to the crowd's demands, releasing Barabbas and sentencing Jesus to crucifixion. Jesus, silent before his accusers, embodies a deep trust in the Father's will, a surrender that transcends human understanding.

The soldiers' mockery, dressing Jesus in a purple robe and crowning him with thorns, aims to humiliate him. Yet, within their cruel actions lies an ironic truth—they proclaim Jesus's kingship even as they seek to degrade, mock, and humiliate him. The soldiers fail to see this irony: Jesus isn't just the King of the Jews; he's the Lord of an eternal kingdom, the sovereign over all humanity, and the King of all creation. Jesus's silence in the face of such cruelty speaks volumes about his surrender to the will of God, his determination and strength, and his profound love for humanity.

This passage invites us to reflect on our response to the humiliated, suffering, and crucified Christ. Will we join with those who crucified Jesus by rejecting his sacrifice, lordship, and love? Or will we surrender our lives to Jesus in love, just as Jesus offered his life to God in love? Furthermore, Jesus's example challenges us to embrace our trials with trust and surrender, knowing that God's love and justice will ultimately prevail. As we follow Jesus, we will face persecution, trials, and suffering. Yet, in our pain, we are united with Christ, finding strength in his presence and courage in his example. May we learn to endure our sufferings with a heart full of love and trust, following Jesus's path of humble and silent strength, and surrendering to the will of God the Father with faith, hope, and love.

Big Idea: Jesus's crucifixion, through profound suffering and ultimate humiliation, reveals the depth of his love for humanity and faithfulness to God. He showed us the way of salvation, forgiveness, humility, and discipleship.

Reflection: How does understanding the full extent of Jesus's suffering and humiliation deepen my appreciation of his love for me? How can I respond to Jesus's sacrificial love, especially when faced with suffering or humiliation?

Prayer: Lord Jesus, in your suffering and silence, you paid the price for our sins and rebellion, offering your body and spirit to God in a profound act of sacrifice and love. You showed us the path of true strength and trust and how to give everything to God as we follow God's will. Please help us to endure our trials with faith, knowing that your love and justice will prevail. We pray, "Let your Kingdom come. Let your will be done, on earth as it is in heaven" (Matt 6:10). Please fill our hearts with your peace and guide us to follow your example, surrendering to God's will with unwavering trust. Amen.

Day 50

Living the Resurrection Hope

Mark 16

There is no resurrection without crucifixion. The resurrection, ascension, and glorification of Jesus Christ needed to follow the path God had laid out for him: birth, baptism, ministry, transfiguration, passion, crucifixion, resurrection, ascension, and glorification. The cross and crucifixion of Christ achieve atonement for sin, reconciliation with God, victory over sin and death, the demonstration of God's love, and the inauguration of a new covenant. But the cross is only the beginning; its meanings are fulfilled in the resurrection. The resurrection achieves victory over sin and death, inauguration of the new creation, hope of resurrection for believers, renewal of all creation, defeat of Satan and evil, confirmation of Jesus's teachings, and new life in Christ. We enjoy all that the sacrifice of the cross and the power of the resurrection have to offer.

In Mark 16, we encounter the heart of the Christian faith—the resurrection of Jesus. Early on the first day of the week, Mary Magdalene, Mary the mother of James, and Salome come to the tomb to anoint Jesus's body. They are burdened with grief, wondering who will roll away the stone. To their astonishment, they find the stone already rolled away and an angel proclaiming,

"He has risen! He is not here" (v. 6). Imagine their surprise! Their Lord and Messiah has risen from the dead, and even the angels tell of his triumph.

This moment of divine surprise transforms their sorrow into overwhelming joy and awe. The resurrection is not just an event but an invitation to live in the light of new beginnings and unending hope. Jesus's victory over death shatters the finality of the grave, offering us the promise of eternal life. Jesus offers us the fullness of life in the here and now and eternal life when God restores and redeems all humanity and creation.

We often carry stones of despair, doubt, and fear as we go through life. Our anxieties and insecurities weigh us down, and we struggle with guilt, loss, inferiority, and sometimes even hopelessness. But the resurrection offers us the fullness of life and, even more, access to God's resurrected life. The resurrection calls us to believe in the power of God to roll away these stones, transforming our darkest moments into opportunities for renewed faith and joy. It challenges us to live as resurrection people, embodying the hope and love of the risen Christ in our daily actions. As we reflect on the empty tomb, let's embrace the call to live with courage and joy, knowing that in Christ, death is defeated, and life eternal is ours.

As the paschal greeting and response say: "Christ is risen! He is risen indeed!" And the angels proclaim, "Don't be amazed. You seek Jesus, the Nazarene, who has been crucified. He has risen. He is not here. Behold, the place where they laid him!" (v. 6). We, too, can live in the hope, life, power, and joy of the resurrection.

Big Idea: The resurrection gives us unending hope, inviting us to live fully in the light of Christ's victory over sin and death.

Reflection: What stones of despair and fear do I need to trust God to roll away in my life? How can I embody the hope and love of the risen Christ in my daily actions?

Prayer: Risen Lord, you offer us unending hope and new beginnings in your victory over death. Roll away the stones of despair and fear that burden our hearts. Please help us to embrace the fullness of life you offer, living each day with the courage and joy of your resurrection. May your triumph over the grave transform our darkest moments into opportunities for renewed faith. Guide us to embody your love and hope in all we do, shining as resurrection people in a world that needs your light. Amen.

Appendix 1

Daily Devotions with Jesus
Devotional Books and Podcast

Daily Devotions with Jesus aims to help you understand and respond to the Bible, grow spiritually, and learn how to impact the world as a follower of Jesus Christ. After all, these devotions aren't just about learning about the Bible. They are also about growing ever more deeply in love with Jesus and following him with every fiber of your being and in every area of your life.

The Daily Devotions with Jesus devotional books and podcast offer a rich, engaging, and spiritually nourishing experience.

Podcast Links:

https://linktr.ee/dailydevotions

https://grahamjosephhill.com/devotions

https://www.youtube.com/@GrahamJosephHill_Author

Features:

The Daily Devotions with Jesus podcast offers a wide range of engaging and beneficial features:

1. **Daily Episodes:** Each episode, lasting around ten minutes, focuses on a specific Bible chapter or set of

verses. Each episode offers a devotion designed to enrich your spiritual life.

2. **Covering the Whole Bible:** The episodes move through the Bible, from Genesis to Revelation.

3. **Guided Prayers:** Each episode offers a prayer tailored to the day's Bible reading, encouraging spiritual growth and personal reflection.

4. **Flexible Pace:** The podcast offers relaxed and flexible pacing, allowing you to go deeper into each chapter or set of verses.

5. **Devotional Books:** You can also get the devotional books accompanying this podcast, which are excellent for individual and group study (see https://grahamjosephhill.com/books).

6. **Bible Reading Plan:** You can follow the Bible Reading Plan at https://grahamjosephhill.com/biblereadingplan.

7. **Listening Options:** To listen on a range of podcasting platforms see https://linktr.ee/dailydevotions.

Appendix 2

Bible Reading Plan

GRAHAMJOSEPHHILL.COM/ BIBLEREADINGPLAN

This Bible Reading Plan shows you how to read the entire Bible, exploring each chapter's themes in depth.

Each day you will read a chapter or set of verses and the devotional book dedicated to the book of the Bible you're reading and you can tune into the accompanying Daily Devotions with Jesus podcast episode.

Tips for Staying on Track:

1. **Keep the Goal in Mind:** The goal is to grow ever more deeply in love with Jesus and follow him with every fiber of your being and in every area of your life.

2. **Set a Specific Time:** Dedicate a specific time of the day to read and listen to the podcast episode.

3. **Reflect and Pray:** Take time to reflect on the chapter or set of verses and pray.

4. **Keep a Journal:** Note down your thoughts or insights from each day's reading.

5. **Seek Understanding:** If a chapter or set of verses are difficult to understand, consider consulting the Daily Devotions with Jesus devotional book dedicated to the book of the Bible you're reading.

6. **Stay Committed:** It's a long journey but staying committed will be rewarding.

7. **Explore the Bible with Others:** Discussing the Bible and devotions in groups can help keep you on track and make your experience more rewarding.

8. **Go Gentle on Yourself:** If you miss a day, go gentle on yourself. You can pick up reading tomorrow. Grace is at the heart of our relationship with Jesus.

The Bible Reading Plan

See the Bible Reading Plan at GrahamJosephHill/BibleReadingPlan. This will be updated as each book of the Bible is completed for the devotional books and podcast.

Appendix 3

Other Books and Resources
by Graham Joseph Hill

Author and Ministry Websites

Linktr.ee/dailydevotions

GrahamJosephHill.com

youtube.com/@GrahamJosephHill_Author

Books

Healing Our Broken Humanity: Practices for Revitalizing the Church and Renewing the World. Downers Grove, IL: InterVarsity, 2018 (with Grace Ji-Sun Kim).

Hide This in Your Heart: Memorizing Scripture for Kingdom Impact. Colorado Springs, CO: NavPress, 2020 (with Michael Frost).

Holding Up Half the Sky: A Biblical Case for Women Leading and Teaching in the Church. Eugene, OR: Cascade, 2020.

Salt, Light, and a City, Second Edition: Conformation—Ecclesiology for the Global Missional Community: Volume 2, Majority World Voices. Eugene, OR: Cascade, 2020.

Salt, Light, and a City, Second Edition: Ecclesiology for the Global Missional Community: Volume 1, Western Voices. Eugene, OR: Cascade, 2017.

The Soul Online: Bereavement, Social Media, and Competent Care. Eugene, OR: Wipf and Stock, 2022 (with Desiree Geldenhuys).

Sunburnt Country, Sweeping Pains: The Experiences of Asian Australian Women in Ministry and Mission. Eugene, OR: Wipf and Stock, 2022.

World Christianity: An Introduction. Eugene, OR: Cascade, 2024.

www.ingramcontent.com/pod-product-compliance
Lightning Source LLC
Chambersburg PA
CBHW060312100426

42812CB00003B/755